The Anatomy of a Raid

Australia at Celtic Wood
9th October 1917
(The Broodseinde Ridge - Third Battle of Ypres)

To John of Lustliegh, Devon.
(He remembers)

In proud memory of our late fathers who served, and the sixty thousand young Diggers who trod the dusty roads of Flanders and Picardy never to return to Australia.

The Anatomy of a Raid

Australia at Celtic Wood
9th October 1917
(The Broodseinde Ridge - Third Battle of Ypres)

by
Tony Spagnoly

Edited by Ted Smith
with an introduction by
John Laffin.

Multidream Publications Ltd.
BM Centre 652
London WC1. England.
1991

Text © Tony Spagnoly and Ted Smith 1991
Introduction © John Laffin 1991
Maps © Ted Smith
Front cover design by Jim Ludden.
Book structure and design by Ted Smith.

Text typeset in 11/12 point Goudy by Multidream Publications.

First published in 1991
by MultiDream Publications.
BM Centre 652, London WC1. England.

Distribution by :
Spa Books Ltd.
P.O. Box 47, Stevenage,
Herts SG2 8UH. England.

ISBN 1 873249 004

ACKNOWLEDGEMENTS

In compiling this very modest appreciation of the Australian effort at Ypres during October 1917, I will admit to approaching it in a spirit of remembrance and respect to those young men who travelled half a world to fall in Flanders.

I do owe a debt to many friends and organisations and this is comprehensively acknowledged with thanks. To the staff of the Imperial War Museum, Lambeth, London, the Public Records Office, Kew, London and the Commonwealth War Graves Commission, Maidenhead, Berkshire, a special thanks for the courtesy and assistance extended when consulting the various written records, photographs, references and maps held amongst their archived materials.

Bob Butcher, Hon. Editor of *Stand To*, the official journal of the Western Front Association was most encouraging and kindly included my initial article on the Celtic Wood raid in one of its editions. Several delightful ladies were always smilingly available with the typewriter when first drafts were needed and to Joan Gamble from Coventry, Joan Schlewinski from Orpington and Sally Buchan from Oxford I hereby record my grateful thanks. A further debt is owed to my very good friends, Tony Shepherd from Oxford and Tom Gudemestad from Seattle, USA, who have tramped with me many times around the Broodseinde Ridge, deep in debate and discussion about those traumatic days in 1917.

Tony also found the time and made the effort to visit the town of Gawler in Southern Australia to photograph the war memorial and the chapel within which Lieutenant Scott, the commander of

ACKNOWLEDGEMENTS

the raiding party on Celtic Wood, and others of the 10th Battalion A.I.F. are honoured. In Gawler Tony was fortunate enough to make contact with Sergeant Tony Traeger of the Gawler police force who dedicated much of his time to helping with the research on Lieutenant Scott and whose contribution did much to help finalise the work on this book. He, assisted by Mr and Mrs Laurie Ronan of the Gawler Institute, supplied the print of a potrait of the Scott brothers commissioned by their mother Mrs J. Scott in honour of her fallen sons which has hung in the Institute from the early post-war years. John Dray from Devon and Vic Sayer from Whitstable gave me the support and friendly counsel needed to establish the correct military assumptions, and this I gladly accepted from men who had experienced war at the sharp end in Italy and north-west Europe during the 1939-1945 conflict I must not forget the young and talented Mary Freeman from Marlborough for her expert help and advice on the poem *The Broodseinde Ridge* appearing in this book, and I must give thanks to her mother, Pat Freeman, who's contribution of her emotive poem *Ypres, November 11th, 11a.m.* adds to the content of these pages. Gratitude is extended to Mrs Peggy Crowle who kindly gave permission to reproduce the photograph and detailed events leading to the award of the D.C.M. to her late father Sergeant Harry Combes, R.G.A.

I am very much aware of the unstinting advice and knowledge afforded to me by two of our leading historians, John Laffin and John Terraine. Their standing in the field of military writing today is known by anyone remotely interested in the subject, and as well known are their respective positions on the question of the High Command's conduct of the war. Be that as it may, both have been free with their considered comment and support, and my deep thanks and respect go to them both. I also owe a great debt to John Giles the founder of The Western Front Association which he formed to perpetuate the memory of all those who fell during the Great War. He has been helpful and supportive, and it was his very successful books on Ypres and the Somme which provided the impetus I needed to complete this project on Celtic.

Jim Ludden has brought his creative talent to bear in the design

ACKNOWLEDGEMENTS

of the book jacket and David Cohen was always ready and willing to advise and contribute on illustrative and art content. My final acknowledgement must be to Ted Smith who has done most to breath a professional life into this project. From the very beginning his enthusiasm and industry have been apparent. His is the planning, structure and design of the book, as is the photographic research, illustrations and preparation of the maps featured. His field work and back-up research, and particularly the casualty research, together with the many hours spent with me working on maps, photographs and documents, as well as the frequent occasions he has walked the ground with me, has helped and added direction to my efforts. If this little work can be seen to have any merit, then this has been earned by Ted Smith. No words can describe my thanks to Ted, nor to his wife Corinne who, as well as caring for home and family and working at a full-time job, somehow managed to help Ted with his research, spent hours with him and myself tramping the battle area and, at the same time, cared for three young children, all under five years old and all experienced battlefield visitors. Corinne arranged and helped with the proof-reading of the book and generally supported Ted throughout the project!

On reflection though, I can see that the unifying influence and common thread was the Australian soldier, the Digger himself. His bravery, his expertise and, not least, his singular humour - a magical combination!

Quotations from published works have been researched as far as possible, and every effort has been made to trace holders of copyright for permission to use the extracts. If any existing copyright has been overlooked in error, copyright holders are requested to contact the publishers.

A. F. Spagnoly. March 1991 London.

CONTENTS

CONTENTS

LIST OF PLATES

LIST OF PHOTOGRAPHS

LIST OF PLATES

Australian wounded at Windmill Hill (also known as Hill 40).

Examining a deserted German sniper's post at Retaliation Farm.

Between pages 56 and 57
Lieutenant Frank Scott and his brother Lieutenant Cleve Scott.

A machine-gun post in trenches between Flinte Farm and Celtic.

The southern edge of the slope that once housed Celtic Wood.

Lieutenant Colonel Wilder-Neligan's raid headquarters.

Between pages 64 and 65.
The Menin Gate Memorial to the Missing, Ypres, Belgium, 1990.

Names of men of the 10th Battalion A.I.F. on the Menin Gate .

The A.I.F. war memorial, Gawler, South Australia.

The Chapel of Remembrance, Gawler South Australia.

Page 89
Sergeant Harry Combes D.C.M., Royal Garrison Artillery.

Between pages 96 and 97.
Halfway House.

The crater and command pill-box, October 1917.

The command pill-box and crater site as it looks today, 1990.

What remained of Zonnebeke Church, October 1917.

Zonnebeke Church and lake, October 1990.

Remi Farm as seen from within the Lijssenthoek Military Cemetery.

Remi Sidings and the road built atop the old railway embankment.

LIST OF PLATES

The China Wall area

Page 106.
Private Reginald Roy Inwood, V.C., 10th Battalion, A.I.F.

Page 107.
Sergeant Lewis McGee, V.C., 40th Battalion, A.I.F.

Page 108.
Captain Clarence Smith Jeffries, V.C., 34th Battalion, A.I.F.

Page 110.
Part of the Hillside pill-box defences.

Between pages 112 and 113.
German strongpoints Hamburg and Beecham.

Defy Crossing.

Remnants of the famous bunker at Hillside Farm.

The low ridge that was the 2nd Objective on the 12th October 1917.

Zonnebeke Church from the Broodseinde Crossroads, 1990.

Divisional dump at Birr Cross Roads.

The divisional dump area at Birr Cross Roads today.

Australian wounded at a Collecting Post on the Menin Road.

LIST OF MAPS

XIV

PREFACE

One of the definitive accounts of the great battles for the Passchendaele Ridge which raged around the Belgian town of Ypres for the latter part of 1917 was written in 1959 by an American historian. He used some very telling word pictures of the pain and suffering, describing scenes which he said would haunt Western civilisation for generations. For the 9th October 1917 he details a major corps attack by British and Australian infantry across the devastated and waterlogged battlefield from the Gravenstafel ridge upward towards the village of Passchendaele itself. This attack, carried out in an heroic fashion by all who took part, was not a success, due in the main part to a stern German defence system and quite hopeless conditions underfoot. Even to emerge from their muddy trenches and to launch themselves forward under a withering hostile fire in horrendous weather was to the eternal credit of the attacking troops, especially when considering that this would be for many of them the first time in action.

As if this level of bloodletting was not enough, the planners threw in less than one hundred young Australians slightly to the south of Broodseinde in an attempt to convince the Germans to spread their counter-battery barrage away from the area of the main advance. This was to be a raid in strength on a small woodland known as Celtic Wood, a well fortified area just south-east of the notorious Broodseinde Crossroads. This raid was referred to briefly in the book and was covered within three to four lines.

This cryptic reference to Celtic Wood with no details or embellishments was the first indication that such a spot in the Ypres Salient existed. It inspired an initial interest to try to find out more of what occurred on that fateful day of the 9th October 1917. On the morning of that day a small party of young Australians advanced into the mist and fire during an action on the Broodseinde Ridge and, for the most part, did not return.

Details, searched for in a multitude of reference and history books relating to the period, are scarce. The trail seemed to go cold at every turn and for many years the mystery of Celtic Wood lay quiet and fallow before opportunity presented itself to enable time to be devoted to the project.

Research into official histories, battalion diaries and numerous books and accounts on actions by supporting and neighbouring battalions revealed little or nothing to supplement or add to the already scant detail. The bare facts were there to digest and the raid plan and accompanying battle map clearly defined the objectives and methodology. The results as recorded in battalion, brigade and divisional reports give a minimum of information and a decisively incomplete record of the event. This lack of worthwhile information prompted concern as to how it was possible for those in command at the time to neglect to investigate, even in the turmoil of post-action activities, the fate of a group of men, no matter what the size. Eighty-five men took part in a raid but only forty-three were accounted for. What happened to the other forty-two? No eye-witness ever recorded an explanation, at least not on the Australian side, and official records leave everything to be desired. Numerous visits to the field of action, frequent debate, much research and a number of discussions with the people now living in the farms and dwellings in the area of Broodseinde and the agricultural property that was once Celtic Wood, served only to increase the frustration of not knowing what happened to a group of ordinary men in khaki wearing the sunburst cap badge.

Visiting military cemeteries and memorials, noting the register detail and cross-referencing with archived materials answered some queries, added to the minute fund of information, and further deepened the interest in what seems to be one of the many unsolved mysteries of war.

PREFACE

Many questions still remain unanswered but one in particular is the one that suggests mystery and prompts suspicion of unrecorded deeds - *what happened to a group of Australian infantrymen who disappeared without trace or record?*

Discrepencies in dates and casualty returns recorded at the time prompt further questions - again unanswerable. Nevertheless, these types of errors are maybe to be expected in a pre-computer age and during the trying conditions under which they were made.

One can only hope that the following account exercises a few minds and leaves us to conjecture personally on what might have happened.

Hopefully there will be those that read this book whose desire will have been prompted by motivations other than those of an interest in military matters or events of the Great War. For these readers, concerned only about the fate of a group of young men who tragically lost their lives, we have included a very comprehensive glossary at the end of the book related to places mentioned. To those of us who study, read about, visit or generally take an interest in the Great War, and particularly those who spend time on the subjects of Ypres and The Salient, such names as Hell Fire Corner, China Wall, Tyne Cot, The Menin Gate, Glencorse Wood and the like are almost day-to-day terminology. For those who don't, then those same names can add confusion, if not bewilderment, to what they are reading. We hope the glossary will help to clear that confusion and bewilderment. We have also introduced a map of the area as it is today for those who would wish to visit the area to study and ponder while standing on, or in, the specific sites mentioned in this book.

Tony Spagnoly and Ted Smith
London. 1991

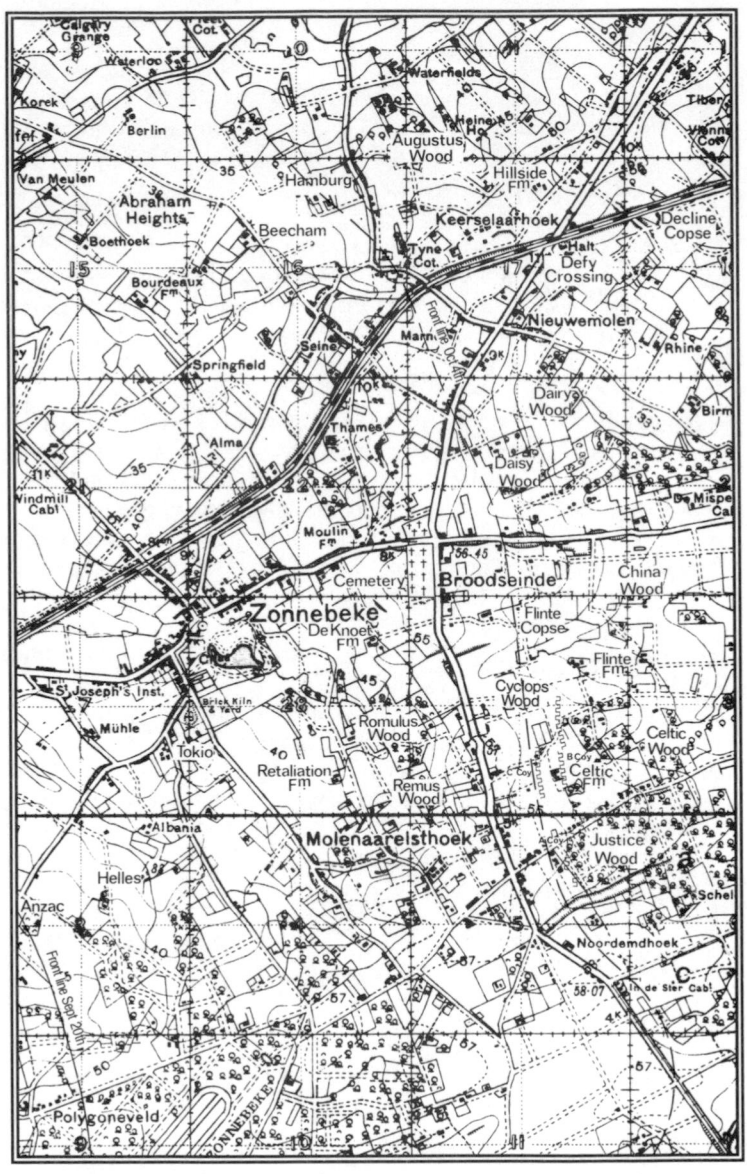

The battle area from Polygon Wood to the Broodseinde Ridge in 1917.

INTRODUCTION

As a boy I grew up among the men whom Tony Spagnoly so much admires - the Australian soldiers of the Great War. My father was one of them, my mother was an A.I.F. nursing sister and their friends were veterans from the war. All had the aura of quiet confidence which comes from maturity, experience and memories. The memories of these young-old men and of their nurses were painful but they never gave way to bitterness. Even the maimed among them - and there were many - did not complain. As volunteers, they had taken their chance and luck had gone against them.

The Australian soldier, the Digger, demanded only a 'fair go'. By this he meant that he expected to be led by officers and N.C.O.'s who knew what they were doing. He also wanted to believe that what he was being asked to do in battle might shorten the war.

When the second Great War broke out in 1939 many Diggers became army instructors to train the new 'Young Diggers' - of whom I was one. Among my instructors were several Ypres Salient veterans and inevitably their training methods leant heavily on what they had experienced at 'bloody Passchendaele.' Not that they wanted us to copy the methods used at Passchendaele - far from it. Passchendaele was held up to us as an example of how not to fight a battle. The Diggers were conscious of having fought and defeated a stubborn and skilful enemy but the cost in life still bothered them. There were too many mistakes, they said.

The raid on Celtic Wood, which has so intrigued Tony Spagno-

INTRODUCTION

ly, was a mistake and Tony explains some of the reasons why it was misjudged. However, in historical terms, it illustrates much about the Diggers and why they were admired by friend and foe. Indeed, many on both sides were in awe of their reckless bravery, boundless confidence and grim determination. All three qualities combined did not produce a successful result at Celtic Wood.

Tony Spagnoly has taken a minor incident of war, examined it carefully and drawn out the human dimension - the effort, the courage, the pain, the loss and, finally, the mystery. Nobody can do more than speculate on the mystery that ended the Celtic Wood exploit and the only solution I can offer is one that I do not care to advance without evidence.

Tony has written his study of Celtic Wood with great sincerity and with an almost devout appreciation of the Diggers. They themselves would say, 'Good on you Tony mate, you've told it the way it was.'

John Laffin

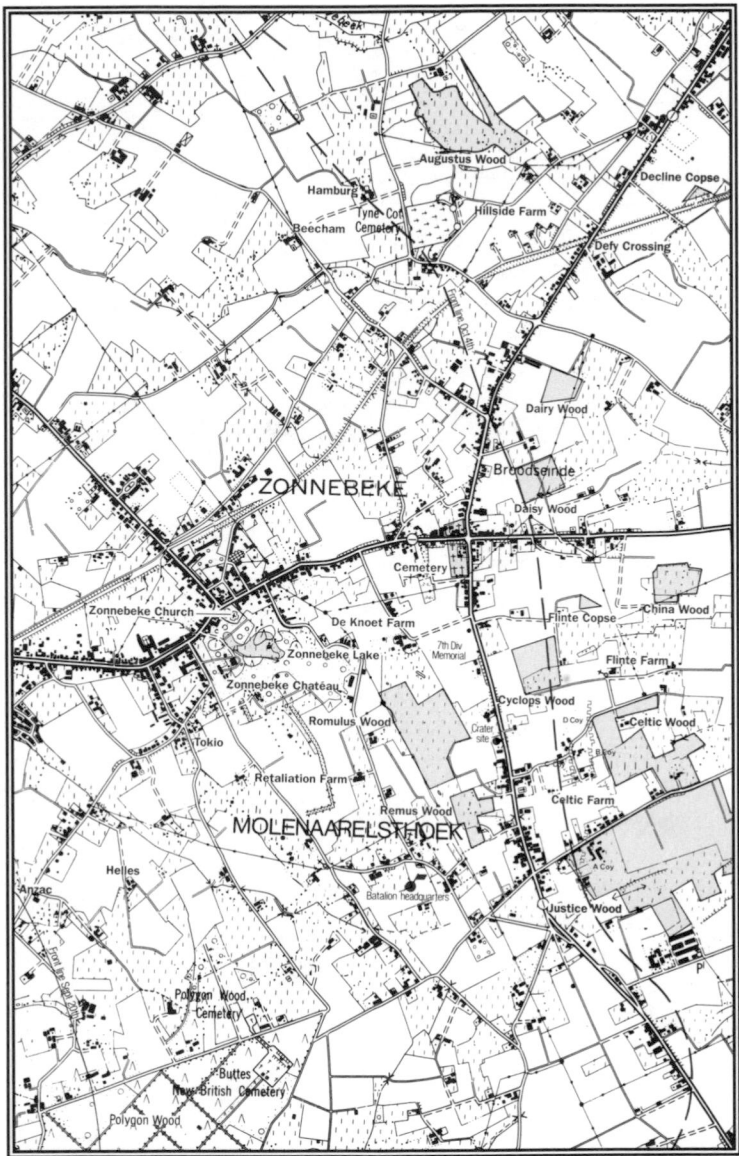

The battle area from Polygon Wood to the Broodseinde Ridge in 1990. For the battle area visitor an enlarged version of this map can be found at the back of this book.

The Broodseinde Ridge 1917 - 1991

The tortured ridge lies gaunt and black
    where blood red poppies grow,
The pilgrim's tread is light upon this sacred ground
    he speaks in tones so low.
By shattered wood and broken cross
    the ravaged willows weep,
Tall as corn came Australia's sons to fall
    and share eternal sleep.

Listen to the mother's cry
    far south in tropic night,
Her sobs unheard beyond the miles
    eclipsed by the savage fight.
Broodseinde will mean naught to her
    as she utters tender sigh,
Proud and strong came Australia's sons
    to climb this ridge to die.

So pilgrim pray the battle's o'er
    and peaceful sun can set,
The ridge lies quiet, a price was asked,
    that price was fully met.
They fell as thick as poppies grow
    and passed with no regret,
With banner high came Australia's sons
    and she will not forget.

                         A.S.

"I think of her so often". A pencil drawing by Balliol Salmon, 1918.

The Broodseinde Ridge.

"Crowded with headquarters and observation posts, it looked out on the famous British salient as on a spread-out map."

C. E. W. Bean.

1
PROLOGUE

"The science of war, its organization and administration, its statecraft, strategy and tactics, are sterile and inoperative without the will and hands of man".

Lieutenant Colonel Graham Seton Hutchison. D.S.O., M.C.

PROLOGUE

O N the 8th October 1917 the staff of the 3rd Australian Brigade, in their shelters around Anzac Ridge near Polygon Wood, must have been surprised to receive orders to mount what would be a second raid within two days on an enemy position named Celtic Wood. This small, heavily defended wood was sited approximately five hundred metres down the eastern slope of the Broodseinde Ridge - a position recently captured from the German army.

The 11th and 12th Battalions from this brigade had already successfully attacked the wood at dawn on the 7th October, gaining valuable identification and information. Now the 1st Australian Division required something more ambitious to support a general corps attack due to start slightly to the north around Gravenstafel and the Abraham Heights. The aim would be to convince the Germans that an offensive would develop on the 1st Australian Division front and make them spread their counter-battery fire all along the line and retain reserves in the southern sector. The brigade's 10th Battalion, men recruited mainly from South Australia, had been rested and trained for such an occasion the preceding week and were selected to execute the raid at dawn on the set date of the 9th October 1917.

When Lieutenant F. J. Scott (Gawler, S. Australia), the raid commander, slipped over the parapet early on the 9th

3

leading eighty-four officers and men of C Company down the gentle slope, through the mist, fire and smoke to enter Celtic Wood, he could have had no conception that he was setting in motion a train of tragic events which the fog of war has shrouded in some mystery to this day.

The raid started successfully, then developed into a fierce hand-to-hand battle, before disintegrating and ending in tragedy. Only fourteen men were able to return to the Australian lines unwounded. To incur seventy-one casualties, or eighty per cent of the party killed, wounded or missing, was a severe enough price to pay even for such a violent clash, but what exercised many minds in the aftermath of the raid when the full story was known, were the following facts, which would indicate that something was amiss, or that, for no apparent reason, the enemy had decided to vary his reporting and recording procedures :

- A list of survivors, wounded or otherwise, was never produced by the enemy.
- A list of prisoners was never provided to the Red Cross - normal practice on these occasions.
- No mention of the raid was made in the defending German battalion's records, the 448th Infantry Regiment, which was somewhat at variance with German military procedures, usually so precise and meticulous in such matters.
- Even more ominous, in the latter part of 1918 when the September battles had cleared the old Salient, grave registration units, who had waited a year to scour the area, found no traces of any bodies or graves to mark the fallen!

The day following the raid, the 10th October, stretcher-bearers under cover of improvised Red Cross flags tried to enter the wood in search of survivors but were fired upon and forced to retire. To all intents and purposes an unknown number of young Australians had disappeared from the face of the earth.

In a conflict which consumed millions, it must be an unprofitable exercise to delve too deeply into one party of missing men however large. Reasons for being reported missing could be many and varied, but in most cases brief enquiries were conducted by those in authority to ascertain the fate of the men involved. For example, during May 1918, men of the 22nd London Regiment (Queens), 47th London Division, successfully raided enemy trenches at the rail embankment, Dernancourt near Albert on the Somme. Five other ranks were unaccounted for and the battalion immediately instigated extensive enquiries until each man's fate had been determined. No such measures seem to have been initiated by the Australian commands in the case of the 10th Battalion and the missing men of C Company.

To be fair, both brigade and battalion dutifully documented the raid, but were in no position on the afternoon of the 9th October to realise the full extent of the tragedy which had befallen their comrades. They wrote :

"The raid has been a great success. Total Australian casualties are forty".

This was probably considered an economical loss rate in view of the size of the raiding party and for attacking the enemy at such a sensitive spot, an area in which the victorious Australian onslaught of the 4th October around Broodseinde had shocked the Germans - a position he assessed as virtually unassailable!

In the fullness of time, those who did not return were classed as officially missing. However, in some small belated gesture of remembrance, it is worth examining in finer detail the events leading up to the Celtic demonstration, and see if they might have a connection or bearing.

"A Lewis Gunner". From a lithograph by Daryl Lindsay.

2

THE BACKGROUND

A Black Day for the German Army.
4th October 1917.

France
4th October 1917

"I have cabled Melbourne to following effect:
'All well, division again brilliantly victorious in 'Greatest
battle of war' … In using the words 'Greatest battle of war' I
quote from a letter the Commander-in-Chief sent me
yesterday"

Major General Sir John Monash.

THE BACKGROUND

OCTOBER 1917 opened with an anticipation that, at last, great things were beginning to unfold. The weather had moderated and the Flemish mud-flats were beginning to dry out. There was a realistic appreciation by Sir Douglas Haig and his two army commanders, Plumer and Gough, that the German armies in Flanders had been dealt some serious and punishing blows, especially since the middle of September on the Second Army front. In the central position I Anzac Corps had punched great holes in the enemy defences at Glencorse and Polygon Woods, advancing over Anzac Ridge just south-west of Zonnebeke (see map facing page 10). A strong German counter-attack south of Polygon Wood on the 26th September had been of brief concern, but even this inconvenience had not prevented the exultant Australians from enjoying a magnificent string of victories, which had seen them capture all their main objectives. This advance had taken them into a sound tactical position around Zonnebeke and the Broodseinde Ridge, ready to develop the next stage of the offensive when required.

Haig correctly elected to stay with the Australians who, rightly or wrongly, from corps commanders downwards, had a general perception that at last the British military planners had improved their performance and got things right.

This, after some ill-conceived adventures concerning Australians at Fromelles and Pozières in 1916, before repeating
the dose at Bullecourt in early 1917. The operations at
Messines in June 1917 had been much better, they thought.
Nothing had been left to chance. Superb planning, master-
ly mining operations, effective use of the artillery and skill-
ful infantry tactics had led to a major victory. Casualties
had been acceptable as British, New Zealanders and Australians had ejected the enemy from his bastion. This had
been a victory as important as Vimy Ridge in April, and the
Germans had been hit hard. Now stage two of Field Marshal Haig's Flanders campaign was well launched. Even
though the August rains and a dogged enemy had slowed
the advance, with British divisions suffering cruel losses, a
change of fortune seemed imminent and the future outlook
augured well. The Field Marshal's bid to gain the high
ground encircling Ypres and break-out beyond before winter
arrived, certainly looked on target after the September fighting. Further crushing blows were in prospect for the German armies as the 4th October approached, but little did
they know it as their high command tried desperately to
keep morale from sagging, and sought ways of restraining
the tide flowing against them.

The 1st and 2nd Divisions of II Anzac Corps that would
assault the hamlet of Broodseinde, perched on its vital crossroads and the ridge stemming south to Becelaere, filed out
from Ypres during the afternoon of the 3rd October and fil-
tered up to their front line, which now lay east of Polygon
Wood. The weather, fickle as ever, had changed to wet and
stormy as the persistent rain began to turn the battlefield
into a quagmire.

Even these dismal conditions however failed to dent the
confidence of the Diggers as they followed their tapes for-

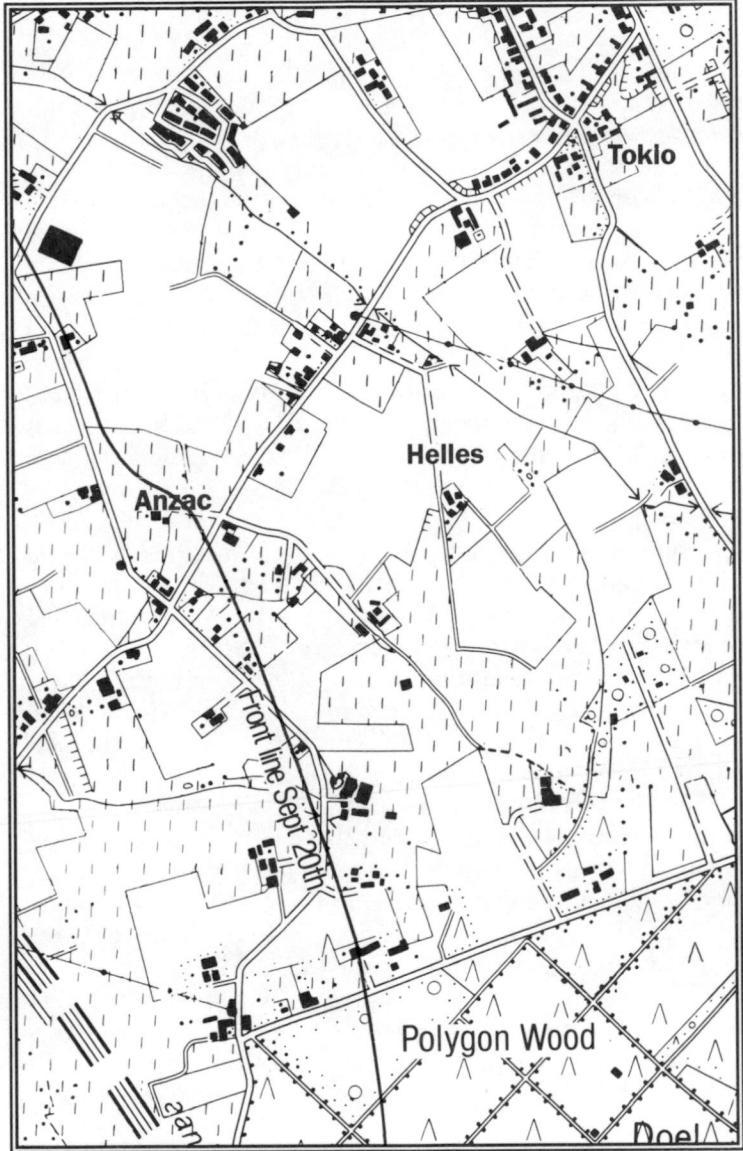

Part of the Australian sector of the front line on September 20th 1917 showing the Anzac Ridge, the Helles Ridge and the Tokio Spur

ward near the Tokio Spur - a slight ridge of high ground due south-west of Zonnebeke (see map facing page 10). They began to lie out in No-Man's Land in advance of their own front line in order to escape the enemy's counter-battery fire which normally descended at the start of any attack.

Unseen before them in the dark along the lower slopes of the Broodseinde Ridge lay several fortified farms the enemy would bitterly contest, including Retaliation Farm and, on higher ground to the north, De Knoet Farm which had a commanding view of all the ground across which the Australians would have to advance. The remains of two small woods named Romulus and Remus clung to the hillside as it rose up to its crest to the main Passchendaele-Becelaere road which ran along it (see map facing).

The Australians planned to attack at 6 a.m., but about 5.30 a.m. as they were quietly waiting, something occurred which caused the more discerning amongst the attackers to arch an eyebrow or two. Desultory German fire which had been falling intermittently among the Australians gradually grew in intensity, alarming many. Observers further back, viewing the fireworks in the darkness ahead, grew tense with worry and anxiety. The enemy fire increased, pummelling the front-line troops before searching and probing for the reserves, transport lines and British gunnery supports further behind the line.[1] Had the enemy anticipated the proposed advance? Was he about to deal out heavy punishment to the vulnerable infantry? More to the point, had he finished falling back, to stand and fight here? The observers watched, quite powerless to intervene. The fire began to take a heavy toll of the waiting men. Casualties were mounting alarmingly. It was anticipated that some units were incurring twenty per cent losses at this stage, particularly in the 2nd and 6th Australian Brigades. After a seem-

(1) Page 85. "SGT. COMBES. D.C.M. ZOUAVE WOOD, 4.10.17"

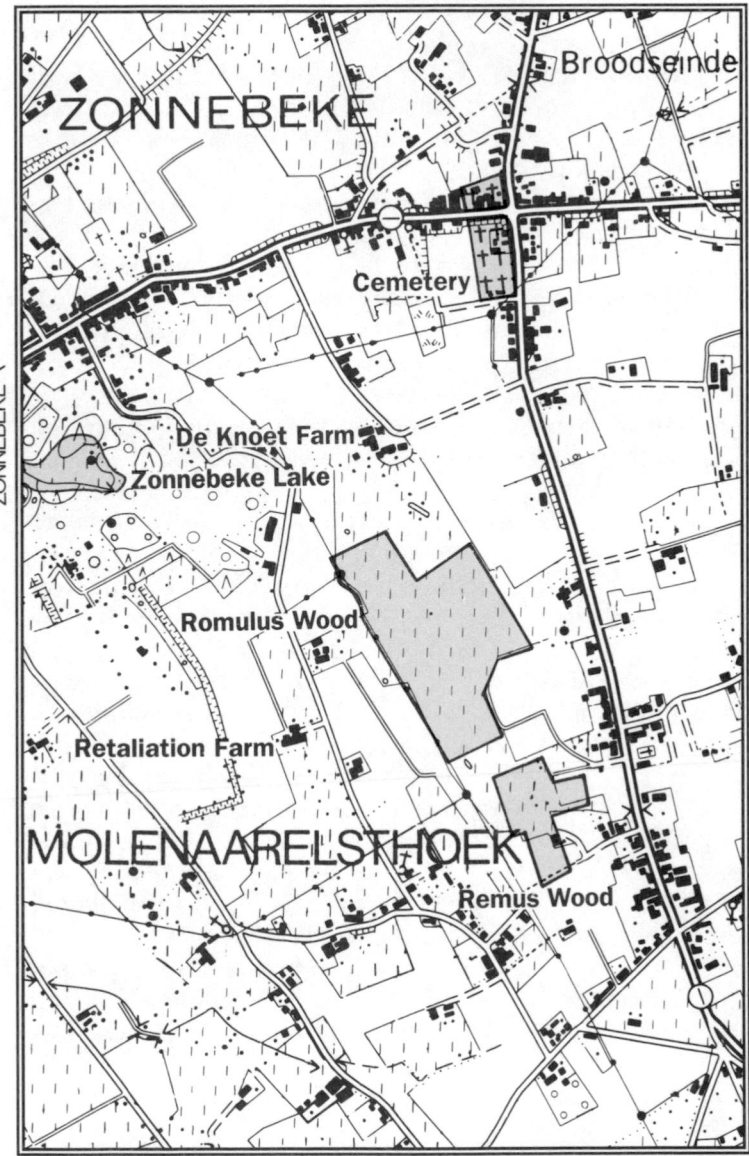

German strongpoints, Retaliation Farm and De Knoet Farm and the fortified Romulus and Remus Woods - all were obstacles to the Australian advance and all saw fierce fighting on 4th October before they were taken.

ingly endless half an hour, the line of the barrage was well
defined by the dead and wounded lying thickly around. The
major worry of course was the loss of so many experienced
officers and non-commissioned officers, the concern being
that, without this reservoir of experience, and with the factor of surprise having been lost, the attack, now nearing zero
hour, may have to be aborted. This then was the major consideration with many senior officers as 6 a.m. approached,
although documents do not show that this thinking had fil-
tered up to any of the main local commanders.

At exactly 6 a.m. a delicate split-second silence was shattered by marker flares sizzling up into the lightening sky.
Then a thunderous British barrage rent the air, drowning
the enemy fire into insignificance. The German positions
all across the ridge were now wreathed in a ferment of fire
and destruction. The Australian infantry, thankful to have
survived the terrible shelling, hoisted themselves off the wet
ground as the whistles blew, relieved at last to be on the
move. Casually, they lit their cigarettes, cocked their steel
helmets against flying shrapnel, gripped their rifles and bayonets firmly and followed their officers into enemy territory.
They were on the move, the Broodseinde Ridge lay ahead.
The enemy gun-fire was now trifling compared to the British barrage and it lessened considerably as the foremost Australians neared the opposing outpost line. As they moved in
from many points from Polygon Wood to Zonnebeke, the
weird shapes of the ruined farms and outlines of the blasted
small woods became discernible as the light improved.

The attackers hurried forward in a bid to keep behind
their protective barrage which was beginning to creep
ahead. Within minutes of the start, when visibility had improved to forty or fifty yards, they stared in disbelief as long
lines of men came towards them out of the mist and smoke.

They looked hard across the cratered ground at the approaching figures, thinking at first that they may be from a
neighbouring unit, but soon recognized them to be German
infantry in the act of launching an attack of their own. The
opposing lines met in the middle of the muddy waste and
one of the quite rare, brutal, face-to-face encounters of the
Great War took place between the lines.[2] The enemy
stopped in their tracks, hardly able to comprehend what was
happening. The Australians were the first to recover and,
shouting and roaring, launched themselves forward. The
Germans turned in a desperate bid to escape up the ridge to
the safety of the defended crest line. Machine-gun fire and
furious bursts from the light field-guns appeared to be chas-
ing their small broken parties all over the ridge slope. Their
losses were extremely heavy as they moved wildly up the
ridge in a frantic attempt to escape lunging bayonets and accurate rifle fire. It transpired later from captured documents
that the enemy had planned a major counter-attack locally
in a desperate bid to recapture some of the higher points of
observation they had lost around Polygon Wood during the
operation of the 26th September. The German attack had
been timed to commence at 6.10 a.m. and the terrible fire
endured by the waiting Australians had been the preparation for this attack. In effect, a ten minute difference in
planning had given the Australians the edge. What would
have been the result if the timing had been in reverse order,
giving the enemy the benefit of momentum and surprise?
Would he have recaptured Polygon Wood eventually?
Would the results of the Third Battle of Ypres have been
different? Who knows what would have happened if the
German had reacted as quickly and as efficiently as did the
Australians on that fateful meeting in No-Man's Land?

Four battalions of the 211th and 212th Infantry Regiment

(2) Page 93. "MAJOR PAGE - A CLOSE SHAVE".

supported by the crack 4th Guards German Division had
been pre-empted by minutes as the Anzacs began their own
advance. What had started out with such high hopes for
the enemy now lay shattered and broken as they retreated
before the rampaging Australians. They were on the run all
along the immediate front. In vain did a few heroic ma-
chine-gunners at sporadic points try to resist. At other places resolute gunners with their light pieces firing over open
sights fought to stem the tide, but the Australians were not
to be denied, and they were certainly not too concerned as
to how they achieved their objectives. The German front
line had been smashed over a two thousand metre frontage.
It was a catastrophic morning for the enemy and more German dead were found in this small area than in any other assault area of the war. Their front line had been overrun and
a large proportion of the dead and wounded had sustained
bayonet wounds testifying to the fierceness of the close combat. The Australians flowed all over the western slopes of
the Broodseinde Ridge neutralising the points of greatest resistance with the bayonet and the hand grenade. Several of
the squat pill-box forts around the ruins of the woods and
the area to the south known as Molenaarelsthoek tried to
hold out. The defenders attempted to break-up the advancing Australians into small parties to separate them from
their protective barrage, but this ploy was unsuccessful.
They were beaten back by the ferocity of the advance. The
Australian infantry, intelligently and courageously led by
junior officers and non-commissioned officers, soon had a
firm grasp on the lower slopes and were beginning to threat-
en the crest line and main road which ran along it.

The main thrust of the advance in this area had been undertaken by the 1st and 2nd Brigades, 1st Australian Division, with the 3rd Brigade in support around Halfway House

and the China Wall area just south of Hell Fire Corner on the Menin Road. No quarter had been asked or given. At places the liaison between the enthusiastic infantry and gunners had broken down as exasperated officers fought to restrain their men advancing through their own protective barrage, now beginning to reduce its fire in preparation for the second stage attack due around 8 a.m. They had to be pulled back to conform with the planned timetable of movement. Some other points saw men from various units breach the crest line and dart across the main road to the reverse slope, only to return reluctantly in case they were caught in the fresh barrage now imminent.

The impetus of the Australian advance had unhinged the Germans' main defences along the ridge and sown panic in their staff, watching with undisguised disbelief from vantage points further east along the Keiburg Spur. As the morning progressed, it became apparent to all that another overwhelming blow had been struck. Any thoughts the enemy staff had of a stand at the highest points of Broodseinde were soon disregarded as they saw the shattered remnants of infantry streaming back down the eastern slopes to the safety of a new line constructed around the complex latticework of small, fortified woods and copses which littered this sector. Army cartographers had accorded names to these woods and would see them flare into a brief prominence, monopolising daily communiques, names such as Celtic, Daisy, Dairy, Decline, and Flinte (see map facing page 18).

As the main force of Australians forced their way up to the higher ground along the crest, rifle and machine-gun fire from strong-points and small pill-boxes unaffected by earlier barrages, spat a venomous fire and threatened to hold up the advance, but small parties of infantry worked their way grimly around the flanks to eliminate these positions from the rear. At the very heart of the German defences were men made of sterner material and stronger measures would be called for. Here the opposition was centred around a large crater at the side of the road, with an excellent field of fire back down the ridge towards Polygon Wood. A large pill-box had been built in this crater with a strong defensive complex of wire and trenches. It housed a local commander's headquarters [3] (see map facing).

This system was garrisoned with senior staff officers, first class non-commissioned officers, determined machine-gun teams and squads of elite Foot Guards. They would make every effort to slow the irresistible tide which was coming to engulf them. The Australians were quick to realise that this resistance would have to be neutralised if the second stage of the advance was to develop safely. Fire from the crater would cause great concern to the advancing infantry. Mixed companies from the 6th and 7th Battalions, 2nd Australian Brigade, crept up to the position, then rushed-in under a fierce hail of hand-bombs and rifle-grenades. Captain H. N. Annear (Creswick and Fitzroy, S. Australia) of the 6th Battalion was witnessed calmly and coolly to reach the crater first. He quickly breached the wire and strode around the crater's edge as if on the parade ground, picking off every officer he could see before he fell mortally wounded.[4]

Both sides fought a violent close encounter before the enemy resistance withered away after suffering heavy losses. One of the 5th Foot Guards senior commanders, Major Wegehaupt, managed to escape down the eastern slopes to the safety of Celtic Wood where he gasped out to stunned colleagues that all their main positions along the ridge had been smashed and completely overrun.

De Knoet Farm, on its knoll near the Broodseinde crossroads, was not allowed to exploit its potential as men of the

---

(3) Page 95. "THE CRATER SITE TODAY".

(4) Page 97. "CAPTAIN H.N. ANNEAR, LIJSSENTHOEK".

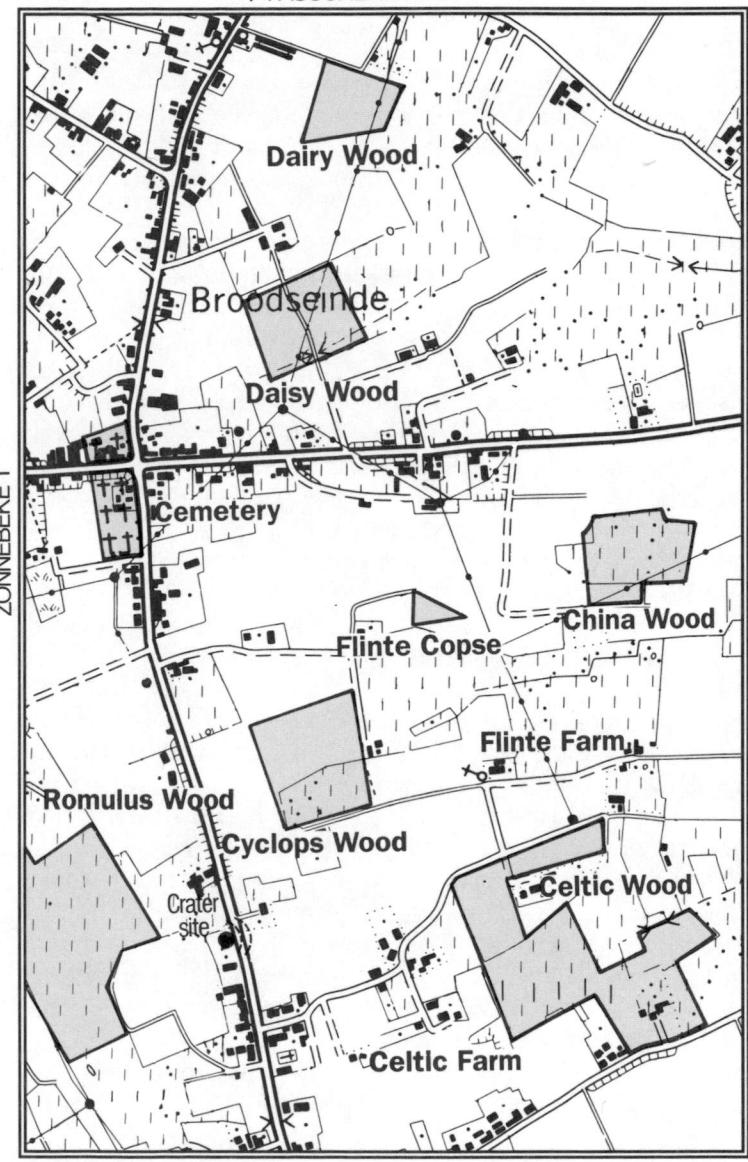

The German fortified woods, copses and farms on the eastern slopes of the Broodseinde Ridge named by army cartographers as Celtic, Cyclops, China, Daisy, Dairy, and Flinte, and the site of the crater on the crest-top road.

21st and 26th Battalions, 6th Brigade, 2nd Australian Division, assaulted with great dash, subduing the garrison at the point of the bayonet and grenade. Several hundred prisoners were taken at this spot. Other men emulated this success above the remains of Remus Wood, overcoming fierce local resistance and going in against machine-guns fired at point-blank range, as German officers frantically tried to work the small artillery pieces sited there. Thus at a most critical period between the first and second stage of the attack, many serious points of resistance had been neutralised so that when the next advance began at 8.10 a.m. the way was clear. The troops, excited with their success, swept over the crest, this time on schedule and in unison.

What a contrast met their tired eyes. Behind lay a foul cratered 'slough of despond', an obscene cesspool which led all the way back to the Menin Gate at Ypres, a veritable 'land of the lost', whilst to the east lay a sight that must have gladdened their hearts. There was a distinct touch of arcady about it all. Green, open fields untouched by the hand of war. Farms and houses with roofs intact and unbroken hedges and fences which had not seen shell or bullet since the opening months of the war three years before in 1914. The possession of the vital ridge which had enabled the enemy to turn Ypres into a hell for the British army had been wrenched from his grasp. The Australians were now well secured on the ridge. Buoyant as they felt, they would now be under an accurate gun-fire orchestrated by the observers on the Keiburg Spur opposite and there would still be local counter-attacks and harassing machine-gun fire to contend with from the defended copses lower down the slopes. Machine-gun fire from Daisy Wood was particularly effective and prevented any further advance from the immediate area of the crossroads. They were happy, however,

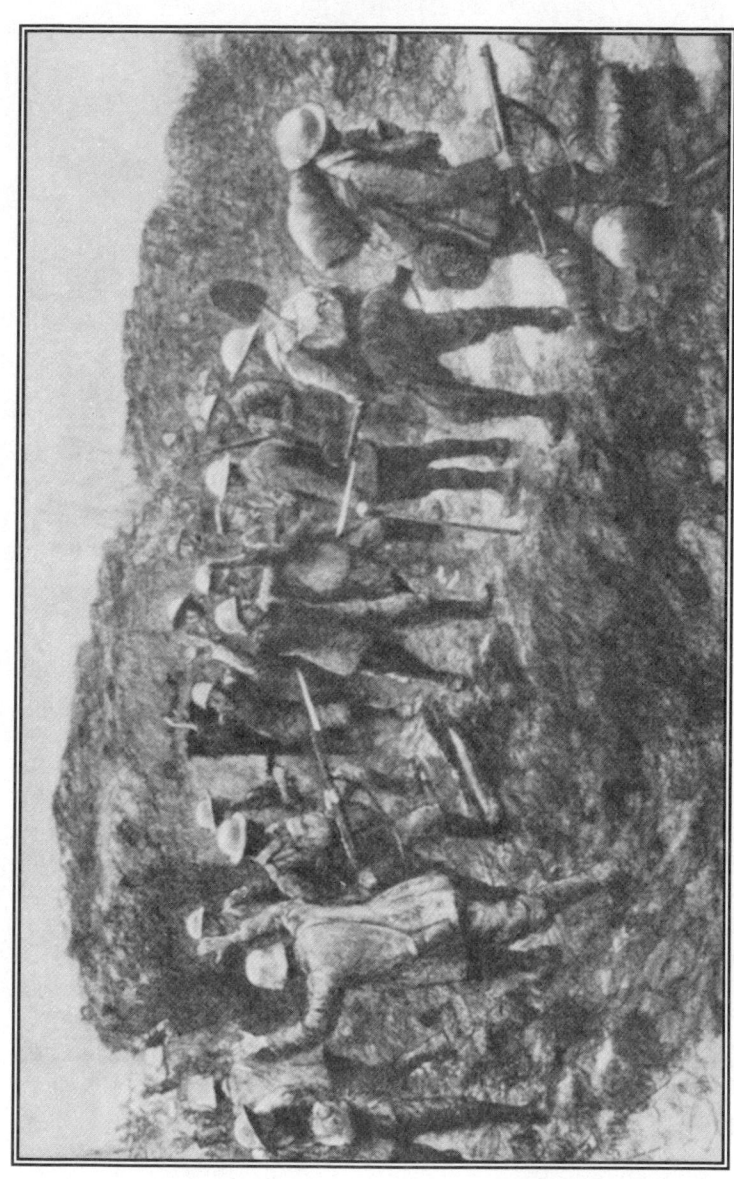

"The capture of a pill-box on the Broodseinde Ridge, October 1917", from an illustration by A. Forestier.

with what they had achieved and would consider the other just a minor irritant, secure in the knowledge of a mighty blow well struck.

German documents recorded the 4th October to be :
"... a very black day in all its magnitude".

Crown Prince Rupprecht at General Staff Headquarters wrote :
"... quite the heaviest battle to date."
and Ludendorff himself wryly observed the battle as :
"... quite extraordinarily severe!"

Steady and accurate sniper fire from the positions ahead did not stop the Australians from strengthening and consolidating the old British 1914 fire-pits which they had utilised when they passed over the crest line. These were sited approximately two hundred metres down the eastern slope of the ridge. These old trenches now came in very useful as the Diggers waited for events to unfold.

As for the German staff away on the Keiburg Spur, they were in a real quandary and could hardly grasp all that had hit them. They had watched in horror as the counter-attack in which they had placed so much trust, was smashed all along the line. They watched powerless to intervene as their men had come streaming back in confusion with their support units annihilated. Uncharacteristically, the Germans had no tabled plan to impede the rampant Australians had the British attack objective been the Keiburg Spur itself. Had this been the case then the continuing and likely success of the Australian advance would have enveloped Passchendaele to their left - and who can tell what course the war would have taken then?

The Australians felt another advance against a dispirited enemy would bear results but were constrained to be patient and continue to conform with headquarter planners. The main actions for the 4th October in this area were now over. It had been a magnificent day and a great achievement for the Anzacs who conceded that Second Army staff had again displayed professional abilities. Sir Douglas Haig himself had wanted to discuss possible exploitation with his Army Commander, Plumer, but with a probable fifteen enemy divisions in reserve he thought it wiser to defeat the expected counter-attacks first. These however were never as intense as expected. Plumer was ready to be persuaded either way, but debate on the amount of artillery required to support a further advance, and the difficulties moving the guns across the lunar, waterlogged landscape finally won the arguments. At 2 p.m. on the 4th October, Field Marshal Haig abandoned any hope of breaking-out locally.

Losses had been heavy for both sides. The Australian Divisions taking part suffered nearly six thousand casualties, many during the barrage on the 2nd Brigade front preceding the abortive enemy attack. Undeterred by these losses, and displaying the verve and spirit which had forged such a reputation since Gallipoli, they had swept away the German waves, gained the ridge top, survived a critical period between the main and secondary attacks, and left a glorious mark along the Broodseinde heights. They had deprived the enemy of one of his greatest bastions encircling Ypres. Apart from the ridge itself, the enemy had lost nine thousand five hundred men on the Second Army front, including nearly four thousand prisoners. Only on the extreme British right near the Menin Road and south of it had the attacks not achieved all the objectives.

Even though the attack would not be developed on this immediate front General Von Kuhl in charge of the German northern armies, admits that the severe fighting of this period had stretched his forces to their limit, gradually forc-

ing the German front at Ypres back on a line about thirty-
three kilometers wide.   But even though the penetration
had been five to seven kilometers deep in places, the British
had not achieved a breakthrough.

   It is a tantalizing thought to consider what might have occurred had the Australians carried on in an easterly direction. With the impetus of their advance behind them, with
good firm ground to advance over, having left the cratered
morass to their rear, and with the Germans hanging on by
their fingertips, who can tell what might have been?

1ST AUSTRALIAN DIVISION
Special Divisional Order. 6th October 1917.
*Though only 10 days have elapsed since the Division distinguished itself
so signally on 20th September, its commander again has to render
thanks and express his gratitude and appreciation for the gallantry of all
ranks in yesterday's successes in this, the greatest battle of the year.*

   *The fortitude of all who participated in the operation since the Divi-
sion took over the line on the 1st inst. under continuous and heavy
shelling, and under exhausting conditions, whether in the line, laying
buried cables, carrying parties, stretcher-bearers, or the pack transport
is beyond praise.*

   *The steadfastness of these battalions who suffered the enemy barrage
prior to zero hour, and yet advanced to the attack and achieved their
difficult objective excites the deepest admiration.*

   *By no means the least gratifying has been the hearty co-operation with
each other between all commands, staffs and Infantry and Divisional
troops. Each and every one was out to forward the general plan, and
right well have they succeeded.*

   *Anzac Landing, Lone Pine, The Somme, Pozières, and here at Ypres
on Sept. 20th (Polygon Wood) and Oct. 4th (Broodseinde) are glorious
records for the 1st Australian Division.*

Sgd.: H. B. Walker. Major General Commanding.

1st Australian Division

"Wounded prisoners October 1917", from a lithograph by Will Dyson.

"The Diggers Prize". From a lithograph by Daryl Lindsay.

3

THE COMMANDERS

A raid is conceived.
8th October 1917.

*"Accordingly in Flanders the struggle went on.
New divisions continued to replace those that were
shattered. The rain descended and the mud sea spread.
Still the power of the Commander and the discipline of the
Army remained invincible"*

The Right Honourable Winston Churchill.

THE COMMANDERS

THE great success of the 4th October had added some urgency to the need to continue the pressure. It was decided that I Anzac Corps would hold the recently captured high ground around Broodseinde whilst II Corps, comprising the 3rd Australian Division, the New Zealand Division and the 49th and 66th British Divisions, would carry the next stage from Gravenstafel onwards and upwards towards the high point - Passchendaele. There would be no tanks due to the extreme bog that existed on the battlefield. Gough's Fifth Army would drive away in the north to breach the Flanders defence line from Spriet, near the Houlthurst Forest, to Westroosebeke, whilst the II Anzac Corps of Plumer's Second Army maintained the aforementioned plan. Ludendorff refers to this period thus :

"The wastage in Flanders was extraordinarily high".

Intelligence had revealed to the British that nine enemy divisions had been smashed from Gravenstafel to Broodseinde by the 4th October assault. Field Marshal Sir Douglas Haig believed that, if the momentum could be kept up, their reserve situation, together with the limitation of the rail system around Roulers, would mean that the Germans would be unable to maintain sufficient troops in the front line. Therefore, to keep the Germans off-balance with no time to recover, Sir Douglas developed the next stage of his

29

offensive by advancing by twenty-four hours his attack to the morning of the 9th October, to be followed three days later on the 12th with another tremendous blow to secure Westroosebeke which linked with Passchendaele on the ridge line.

It is now known that at this stage Crown Prince Rupprecht considered drawing back to a shorter line in Flanders, and was planning this very move when the gods of war contrived to come to his rescue in the form of a change in the weather. The rain was now quite relentless, soon turning the battlefield into an even more indescribable and impassable morass. The weather deteriorated so much between the 4th and 7th October with cold, squally rain that all concerned became dispirited and depressed.

That day the two army commanders informed the Commander-in-Chief that, although willing to continue, they would not be unhappy if the campaign was suspended for the winter. Sir Douglas indicated that he would wish to continue at least until the Germans were ejected from the highest ground which afforded so much domination. He was worried that the longer his blow planned for the 9th October was delayed the better chance for an enemy, known for his resilience and dogged defensive capability, to recover. His other concern, quite rightly, was that a premature close-down of the campaign would allow the enemy the opportunity to divert valuable troops to other areas in the south where they might have a decisive effect. In these circumstances therefore he was most anxious that the attacks planned for the 9th October should not be postponed. As the 9th approached the weather which had fluctuated for days was still severe, and the forecast showed no great improvement in the short term.

In pouring rain therefore, the attacking brigades began

their move up the line. The approach roads began to break up after the frenetic activity and loads of the past two weeks. Three weeks of persistent shelling had blocked the water-courses and the many thousands of shell holes prevented efficient drainage. The area behind the attacking II Anzac Corps, in the valleys of the Steenbeke and Strombeke, was described as *"a vast porridge of mud"* and tremendous difficulties were encountered getting the required number of guns up in close support across the gloomy desolation. Unstable platforms saw many pieces sink into the mud up to their axles, and some even to the gun muzzles. Their target range was an extreme one of six thousand yards, ranging on the ruin of Passchendaele church. Behind I Anzac Corps, whose role would be a holding one slightly to the south, the conditions were only marginally better. Their guns would be a mile behind their front line, but the approach 'duck-walk' tracks over Anzac Ridge and those of the Helles Ridge, just to the east, had already broken under the traffic, and many guns were left stranded.

In the vast wilderness before II Anzac the view was of slime and mud, with no hedge, building or shelter in sight as again the troops just waited, exposed to the elements. To contemplate an attack in these conditions, let alone execute one, would be to the immortal credit of the British and Australians involved. It was obvious that every effort would have to be made to convince the enemy to spread his fire away from the mass of attackers around Gravenstafel Ridge. A demonstration in strength on the I Anzac front at Broodseinde might do the trick in ensuring that the Germans would suspect another major probe in that sector too. Thus fire and reserves might be kept away from the main area of advance at a critical time.

The 1st Australian Division were made familiar with the

assessment, and it was this sequence of events that saw orders arrive at 10th Battalion headquarters on the 8th October via 3rd Brigade that they would, under a protective barrage, launch a company raid at dawn of the 9th on Celtic Wood.

Even as the messages began to flow between 3rd Brigade at Halfway House, just south of the Menin Road, and the 10th Battalion who were now lying below the ridge at Broodseinde, the weather was always the immediate concern of the commanders and senior observers preparing for the main 9th October attack.

John Terraine, the eminent historian, in his detailed scrutiny of the campaign, *The Road to Passchendaele*, quotes from a letter by Sir Douglas Haig to Lady Haig on the 8th October in which he states :-

"Bright and clear with a high wind which is drying the ground nicely. But yesterday's rain made the mud very bad beyond Ypres in the low ground, and stopped all the guns we wanted getting forward, but we have enough for tomorrow's attack."

Whilst early next morning on the day of the attack, the 9th October, the Field Marshal notes in his personal diary :-
"Gale blew all night. Morning very windy but fine."

Even though the weather would have a considerable affect on the proceedings, hopes of a further advance were high. German fire notwithstanding, the further obstacles of wire, mud, rain and the cratered ground would not impede this further attempt to gain the upper reaches of the Passchendaele Ridge, a sound winter line, and the added bonus of taking pressure off their French allies to the south.

Brigadier General Charteris displays all this optimism through gritted teeth on the 8th October when he wrote :-
"We go on again tomorrow, and yesterday and today there has been heavy downpours, a last effort. Documents taken on the

IWM E(Aus)9166

Looking toward Glencourse Wood and Inverness Copse during the German counter-attack, 26th September 1917. This area had been held by the Germans in spite of heavy attacks by the British 56th and 18th Divisions in August 1917. It fell to the Australians in their Menin Road offensive of late September 1917.

The German pill-box which gave its name to the Anzac Ridge. This prominent structure was captured by infantry of I Anzac Corps during the opening stages of the Menin Road battles in late September 1917. It was while in shelters on this ridge that staff of the 3rd Australian Brigade on the 8th October 1917 received orders to mount the raid on Celtic Wood the following morning.

Anzac Ridge with strongpoints of a more peaceful nature, 1990.

Ted Smith

The crest of the Broodseinde Ridge today, above De Knoet farm and looking south from the left of the 7th Division Memorial. The Australians swept over this ridge from right to left on the 4th October 1917. The command pill-box and crater site are just above the slope of the road as it veers right behind the tree foliage. In the distant left the houses of Molenaarelsthoek can be seen, once described as *"teeming with forts and pill-boxes"*. The slope leading down to the site of Celtic Wood begins to the left behind these houses.

IWM E(Aus)1914

Tokio Spur. The Australians laid out in No-Man's Land in front of this ridge before they advanced on the morning of 4th October 1917. It was from here that they suffered heavy casualties in the early dawn when caught in the German preparatory barrage.

Dead Germans near Retaliation Farm after having met with the Australians in No-Man's Land on the morning of the 4th October 1917.

Australian wounded at Windmill Hill (also known as Hill 40), an Advanced Collecting Post near Zonnebeke railway station, after the successful assault on the Broodseinde Ridge, 4th October 1917.

IWM E(Aus)4503

An Australian officer of I Anzac Corps examining a deserted German sniper's post at Retaliation Farm, 17th October 1917. This farm and its surrounding area saw much of the hand-to-hand fighting on the morning of the 4th October.

4th show the Germans are very hard pressed to hold their ground.
They have given up their new plan of thinly held front lines and
gone back to their old scheme, which is all to the good, but unless
we have a very great success tomorrow, it is the end of this year
as far as Flanders is concerned, and next year the Germans will
have their troops from Russia. With great success tomorrow,
and good weather for a few more weeks, we may still clear the
coast, and win the war before Christmas!"

In the meantime the men of the 10th Battalion selected as
the raiding party were concerned with their own, rather
more modest objective, the forthcoming raid on Celtic
Wood. The commander of the Battalion at the time, Lieutenant Colonel M. Wilder-Neligan, started life in the English Devon county town of Tavistock in 1893. He was in
Australia at the start of the Great War and joined the ranks
of the Australian Commonwelth Military Forces in southern Australia. He landed at Gallipoli as a sergeant in the
9th Battalion, 1st Australian Division and soon became not-
icable for his resourcefulness and for his traits of leadership
during a daring seaborne raid down the coast from Anzac
beach. He was soon to be awarded a battlefield commission.
He spent time in the Sinai desert, building on his experience for commanding men and organising patrols, before ar-
riving in France with the Division. He soon made a name
for himself in the Fleurbaix and Fromelles sectors by planning and executing a number of successful raids. He was an
adventurous and well thought of soldier, rigid when it came
to discipline, but devoted to his men and meticulous in his
planning. The men in turn gave him their loyalty, admiration and respect, and this from soldiers who did not accord
these values lightly is possibly the surest indication of his
natural flair for leadership.

He is classed by Dr. C. E. W. Bean who documented the

exploits of the Australian Infantry Force in France and Flanders during the 1914 - 1918 conflict, as being among the best leaders of infantry produced by Australia during the war.

Lieutenant Colonel Michael Wilder-Neligan, C. M. G., D. S. O., D. C. M. took command of the 10th Battalion in the summer of 1917. He survived the war and returned to Australia with the main force of the military after the Armistice.

4

A RAID IS PLANNED

8th October 1917.

SECRET.

Tenth Infantry Battalion A. I. F.
Order for raid on CELTIC WOOD.

1. Intention. "C" Company, 10th. Battalion plus reinforcements will raid that part of CELTIC WOOD between D.30.C.00.65 to D.29.D.8.6. to D.29.D.7.5. to D.29.D.75.35. to D.30.C.00.45.

Document No.130. Public Records Office, Kew, London.

A RAID IS PLANNED

THE 10th Battalion was an experienced unit of men recruited mainly from South Australia. They formed part
of 3rd Brigade, a formation who had missed most of the traumatic events of the 4th October. They were acting as divisional reserve at Halfway House and the China Wall position close to Hell Fire Corner when their colleagues of the
1st and 2nd Brigades had captured the ridge. They had relieved the units in the front line and were now responsible
for holding the ground gained. The 10th had seen plenty of
action since 1915 and, as recently as September, they had
played their part in the capture of Polygon Wood, receiving
two hundred and fifty casualties in the process, including
seventy-two killed and missing. Private Roy Inwood had
gained a Victoria Cross on the 21st September in a gallant
attack on a machine-gun post which threatened the advance.[5] To recuperate from their losses, and to integrate
reinforcements into their depleted ranks, they had been in
the Steenvoorde area until returning to divisional reserve at
China Wall for the Broodseinde battles on the 1st October.
To indoctrinate such a large number of new men into the
life and lore of a battalion takes time, and time on the Ypres
front at this period was in short supply. This would be the
first time in action for many of the new men. Between the
7th and 8th October the 10th Battalion found themselves

37

(5) Page 101. "AUSTRALIAN V.C.'S SEPT. - OCT. 1917".

in make-shift fire trenches near Remus Wood on the western slope of the Broodseinde Ridge, less than six hundred metres from their raid objective, Celtic Wood, down the eastern reverse slope.

Unknown to the Australians, Celtic Wood was now packed with defenders due to the effect of a dawn raid by their 11th and 12th Battalions on the 7th October, set up to obtain identification of the unit opposing them. Two officers and thirty other ranks from the 11th Battalion and one officer and thirty-seven other ranks from the 12th had struck quickly as light broke and surprised men of the German 448th Infantry Regiment, part of the 233rd Division who had recently moved from the St. Quentin area to help make up some of the losses incurred since the British Third Ypres offensive had begun. The 448th were new to the area and were unprepared as the Australians attacked, leaving twenty enemy dead in their wake, capturing a machine-gun and hustling fifteen prisoners over the wire and back to the Australian lines before the Germans had realised what was going on. It was all over in twenty minutes and the exuberant Anzacs had only two men wounded in the fracas.[6] However, the raid had alerted the enemy and the wood was now packed with grim and determined men awaiting the next move from the Australians confronting them. They would be intent on retribution for the indignities suffered by the Imperial German Army over the past weeks.

This was the mood then along these historic slopes, as the 10th Battalion under Lieutenant Colonel H. Wilder-Neligan prepared for the second sortie on Celtic Wood. If anyone was puzzled or troubled by a raid at the same spot after such a short interval, no papers exist today in the available archives to support such a contention.

The reason given for the raid was to support the main at-

---

(6) Page 113 - "RAID REPORT - 11TH/12TH BATTALIONS, 7/10/17".

tack by a neighbouring corps, but in reality most of the battalion would retain a defensive flank along the Broodseinde Ridge whilst the raid was executed at one company level.

The motive of the raid was mainly to persuade a watchful and wary foe to spread his fire and retain reserves at Broodseinde away from II Anzac who would have troubles severe enough of their own beyond the Gravenstafel Ridge. That was the main consideration of Wilder-Neligan as he called in his company commanders on the evening of the 8th to discuss the plan. The objective and orders for the raid are set out in the raid plan, document No. 130 signed by the battalion commander, now among the battalion papers in the Public Records Office, Kew, London.[7]

C Company was chosen to execute the raid under the leadership of Lieutenant F. J. Scott. Four parties of two officers and twenty-five other ranks were originally proposed but, in the short interim period since the order was made, sickness and battle casualties suffered in just holding the dangerous and exposed ridge, had reduced the force to five officers and eighty other ranks. The men would attack with small arms but the raid plan made provision to receive trench mortar and Light Artillery support from 5th Australian Division gunners.

The other companies would be deployed and assist with covering fire. C and D companies would interchange just before the raid, whilst A Company would provide a block to the south nearer the hamlet of Noordemhoek, to prevent interference from that direction.   Battalion machine-guns would provide a flanking fire for the raiding party whilst they were in the wood and stop infiltration by other neighbouring units of the enemy. The document stated :

"… this operation would assist the major plan being activated in the north".

(7) Page 121. - "DOC. 130 - THE RAID PLAN, 10TH BATTALION".

It would be carried out at 05.20 a.m. on 9th October 1917. Map: Zonnebeke Sheet 28 NE. Squares D29D and D30C. (see battle map facing).

That was the simple plan. That was the composition of the party. All was now ready for the signal.

After two days of gale conditions and continuous rain, the early dawn of the 9th October was breezy but dry as the men of the 10th Battalion filed confidently from their position on the western slopes of the Broodseinde Ridge, just above Remus Wood, across the crestline and down the reverse slopes to the fire trenches reserved for them.

In the strange pre-attack quiet, interrupted by the odd gun firing here and there searching the line, their battalion comrades from the other companies would have patted the backs of the men of C Company, who would have been preparing themselves mentally for the task ahead, wishing them well in lowered tones and joking of the hearty breakfast they would enjoy together on their return, in *"Zero plus 30 minutes"* as the attack plan indicated.

That *"30 minutes"* would prove to be an eternity for most of the young men now preparing to face the fire from Celtic Wood as they filed quietly over the main road topping the crest of the Broodseinde Ridge to take-up their positions in trenches down the misty eastern slope. The die was cast. Now the machinery of war would take its course.

5

THE RAID

9th October 1917.

"... at 5.20 a.m. on the 9th October our attack was renewed on a front of over six miles, from a point east of Zonnebeke to our junction with the French north-east of Langemark ... at the same time, minor operations were undertaken on the right of our main attack, ... east and south-east of Polygon Wood"

Field Marshal Sir Douglas Haig's Despatches.

THE RAID

A S Lieutenant Scott led his men into the flame that covered Celtic Wood, his thoughts must have been on
many things other than his so called protective barrage but,
to some Australian observers on the high ground, it seemed
that the artillery support was not coming up to expectation.
Nothing like the expected barrage had been achieved even
though watches had been synchronised and firing had started on time. A battalion verdict later was that :

*"... the barrage seemed thin - and nothing out of the ordinary.
The Germans did not appear bothered by it at all, and seemed
quite unconcerned as the raiders drew near".*

The barrage palled into insignificance at the thunderous
roar which accompanied II Anzac Corps going into action
to the north. If the raid by the 10th Battalion was a ruse to
decoy the enemy into thinking this was part of the main attack, then the sporadic and thin barrage was ensuring that
the German garrison at Celtic Wood and the positions
around would think otherwise. They would sense immediately that this was a 'demo'. In their experience, Australians did not do things by halves, and this effort did seem a
little lack-lustre. German eyes peered up the slope to note
any support for the attackers - there was none. The luckless men of C Company were on their own!

In the earlier stages of the raid the trench mortar fire was

particularly effective and an entry at the northern end of
the wood was successful as the enemy posts began to fall
back. The raiders went in from the west and the north but
the Germans, after an initial hesitancy, gauged this was not
the concerted attack which they feared, but another example of the audacious Australians' attempt to rub their nose
in it for the second time in days. Their resolution began to
stiffen. The Germans had reinforced the area since the 7th
and were certainly more prepared. Heavy enemy machine-
gun fire now began to rake the Australians prowling
through the little wood. Any movement resulted in an effective rifle fusilade from the north-east and a strongly
manned trench sited on a ridge within the wood (marked as
D.29. D. 9. 6. on trench maps of the time). The place was
described by one of the wounded who returned as:
"… teeming with snipers and sharp-shooters".

Estimates afterwards put the defenders as outnumbering
men of the 10th Battalion by over two-to-one. Lieutenant
Scott was seen to urge some of his men forward and deeper
into the wood in a bid to neutralise the effective sniper fire
now taking its toll. Others endeavoured vainly to out-flank
the entrenched German riflemen whilst some, keeping to
the plan, attempted to destroy the many dug-outs and weap-
on-pits. Suddenly, as if a command had rung out, counter-
moves of the enemy went into effect as a fierce barrage cur-
tained-off the wood from observing eyes and effectively
boxed-in the raiders, cutting off any escape route back
across No-Man's Land. This built up into a crescendo as the
frenzied fire drenched the rest of the battalion who, four
hundred metres away, were fearful for the fate of their comrades in the wood. The space between them was impassable
and a line of smoke shells not only screened the watchers
but quickly gave them the impression that the cause of the

eighty-five raiders was lost. The Germans had sprung an efficient response. A supposedly quiet sector was now a small compact hell as the woodland, and the Australians in it, were blasted with fire of all sorts and a fight to the death among the trees now took place. They began to wilt as the enemy fire began to break them down into smaller groups. Only then did parties of enemy infantry, filtering in from the Keiburg Spur when the raid started, begin hunting them down. The Battalion report laconically states that at this stage :

"... the fire was furious - and we were badly outgunned".

It would appear initially that Lieutenant Scott had caused some worry to the garrison which was quite unsure of his overall intention. His probing deeper into the wood, leaving a number of enemy dug-outs and gun positions behind, resulted in many of the raiders, thinking the day was won, following until they almost reached the far end of the wood. They became overstretched and were gradually picked-off by the ever-present enemy, now in superior numbers and confident of the result. Fierce hand-to-hand combat now took place as Lieutenant Scott's short lived mastery began to evaporate under the withering fire. The Australians were trapped, with no way back up the slope to the rest of the battalion and safety. They were cut-off by the excellent enemy counter-battery work and the 5th Australian Division artillery was now noticeably deficient in comparison.

The enemy counter-attacks against the despairing raiders were courageously led by officers intent on settling a score with them and the Australians were now engaged in a fight to the death - split-up into small groups and with no hope of escape. Lieutenant Scott and his small command party were soon engulfed and this brave young officer was seen to fall. Lieutenant A. W. Rae (Kilkenny, S. Australia) was also hit and Lieutenant W. H. Wilsdon (Caltowie, S. Australia) just disappeared and was never seen again.[8]   As the light of day began to strengthen, the furious fire began to fade and the thick smoke slowly cleared over the woodland. The 448th Infantry Regiment were still in possession and Celtic Wood fell quiet again. Its brief prominence over, it now sank back into a quiet sector never to be fought over again. A year later, in September 1918, units of the 9th Scottish Division taking part in the final advance out of the Salient secured the area quickly and were beyond Celtic in minutes.

Attackers in the main northern offensive that the raid was meant to assist had stumbled forward but the two formidable and continuous belts of new wire entanglements, thirty yards in depth protecting the pill-boxes of the Flanders front line in front of Passchendaele, did much to restrict any great success. This was the real obstacle on the 9th October. Conditions were quite lamentable. The sodden battlefield was littered with dead, with the wounded being forced to lie out for up to two nights. Enemy pill-boxes used as shelters were overflowing with unattended wounded and the dead who lay just outside. The survivors huddled together in the desolate wastes under constant fire. It was a dispiriting situation. The Press Corps at General Headquarters were told :
"... mud alone caused our failure on the 9th".[9]

Brigadier General Charteris went further, his confidence of the previous forty-eight hours rapidly evaporating. He wrote on the 10th October :-
"I was out all yesterday at the attack. It was the saddest day of the year. We did fairly well but only fairly well. It was not the enemy but mud which prevented us doing better. There is now no chance of complete success here this year. We must still fight on for a few weeks, but there is no purpose in it now as far as Flanders is concerned."

(8) See Cameo page 107 - 'Officers Wilsdon and Rae'.

(9) Appendix III page 121 - 'Passchendaele - The German perspective'.

6

THE AFTERMATH

10th October 1917.

"... a raid on Celtic Wood by men of the 1st Australian Division found the enemy well prepared, and only 14 of the 85 officers and men engaged returned unwounded"

Official History of the War. Military Operations in France and Belgium 1917 . Volume II.

THE AFTERMATH

LIEUTENANT R. P. James (Renmark, S. Australia) and Lieutenant L. B. Laurie (Salisbury, S. Australia) limped back with twelve other survivors after darkness fell, having lain dormant amongst the slain all through the day. It was all over and the adventure which had started out with such high hopes had ended in disaster. The greater number of the young Australians taking part in the raid had literally disappeared and, even following the conclusion of a bloody fight, this was difficult to explain.

Something quite disastrous seems to have been visited on the luckless men of C Company. Lieutenant Colonel Wilder-Neligan, ever watchful for more survivors during the night, wrote to Brigade early on the 10th October :

"... quite possible that a certain number of the missing are prisoners or are wounded. We are hopeful some may yet come in and be accounted for definitely".

They didn't - and they weren't - ever. Efforts were made to search for wounded in or around the fringes of the wood but, as already stated, stretcher-bearers under Red Cross flags were fired on and forced to retire to safety.

Both the 1st Australian Division and its 3rd Brigade documented the raid in optimistic terms directly after the fight ended, obviously neither fully aware of the tragic casualty list. A clerical error gives the raid date as the 8th instead of

the 9th October in the divisional report which is terse, precise and economical in stating:

*"Our 10th Battalion, co-operating with 2nd Division (on the
left) raided the area of Celtic Wood (Broodseinde). Fierce hand-
to-hand fighting took place in the eastern end of the wood. The
whole wood successfully mopped up. Our losses totalled forty officers and men. No prisoners were taken."*

No prisoners? Who was left to bring any back?

The brigade version, besides being more concerned with
the failure of the supporting gunners, also says :

*"Our casualties were heavy taking into account size of the party.
Forty all ranks! Estimated enemy losses forty dead plus thirty
wounded. Our men found great difficulty in disengaging and
withdrawing up the exposed slope. Many had to stay put in shell
holes and endure heavy enemy shelling all day."*

In the immediate aftermath of the raid the role of the gunners supporting the 10th Battalion was also examined in
sharper detail.[10] Report No. 244 of the 11th October sent
to the 1st Australian Division Headquarters by Brigadier
General H. G. Bennett, commanding 3rd Brigade, complained :

*"Artillery co-operation had not been as good as had been expect-
ed and the operation's success had to be jeopardised. The promised density of the fire had not been attained, leaving the attackers at a disadvantage".*

The report went on to blame the heavy casualties upon
this aspect of the support. This communication wound its
way through official channels to Major General Walker,
General Officer Commanding 1st Australian Division, then
to Lieutenant Colonel J. Peck, the 5th Australian Division
staff officer responsible for the supporting fire. Back came a
speedy defence on the 12th October (document Ref. 124/99
refers) from Lieutenant Colonel Caddy, commanding B

---

(10) Page 129. - "ARTILLERY DEBATE CORRESPONDENCE".

"Australian artillery in action", from a painting by J-J. Berne Bellecour 1917.

Group, 5th Australian Division artillery. In mitigation he said :

"Can understand the whole barrage may not have come up to expectations due to various circumstances (list of provisos tendered) and failure by units of British 7th Division holding southern flanks between Noordemhoek and Becelaere - but the fire patterns laid down around Celtic could not possibly be included in this statement."

As far as they were concerned all that had been arranged and promised in support had been delivered.

The questionable role of the gunners in all this abortive and tragic venture cast gloom and caused not a little recrimination all round, especially between the 1st Australian Division and the 5th Divisional Artillery Commander, Lieutenant Colonel J. Peck.

It would seem that, after the initial flurry of memos and documents, the whole subject was laid to rest. The frantic activity that accompanied the rest of the winter campaign towards Passchendaele no doubt had something to do with this matter being put aside and no further effort was made to resolve the questions raised.

Celtic Wood was quiet again, and those who fell within its confines are consigned to history books. The lessons learned in the Celtic Wood affair may well have contributed to future Australian actions. Who knows whether the 'peaceful penetration' campaign conducted by them with such clinical efficiency in the months following the German March 1918 offensive was not a direct result of experiences at Celtic Wood?

7

THE RESULTS

"... all organizations relieve men of every sort of duty, human, personal, or moral. Therein lies the root of all evil in the world. Men are beaten to death, demoralized, degraded, and nobody bears the responsibility"

Rudolf Binding.

THE RESULTS

THIS episode in *The History of the 10th Battalion A.I.F.* is covered quite tersely within ten lines, giving the date of the raid in the text for some reason as the 10th October, although the diary section of the same history correctly states it as the 9th October. It also states :

"... about nineteen other ranks returned."

It gives only twenty-three names of infantrymen together with three officers who were killed in action on the 8th, another error in the date, without any attempt to clarify the discrepancy. In the battalion diary summary of the action it was judged that :

"Heavy casualties were undoubtedly inflicted on the enemy, and did hold reserves in the area to counter any major attack just as the plan had demanded. Some heavy guns, machine-gun units and extra men had been drawn into the divisional sector which could have been used with value along the Gravenstafel heights. There is no doubt that for a vital hour or so, as the main attack went in along II Anzac Corps front, he was bewildered and torn with indecision as to what to expect in the sector of Celtic Wood".

The report sent on to Brigade then goes on :

"This demonstration would have produced extremely good results, with many prisoners, if the artillery preparation had been even moderately good with far less casualties than we seem to

have taken. The episode has not lowered the morale of our men, if anything it has heightened it, owing to the first hand-to-hand fight they have experienced against an experienced and well entrenched enemy".

This refers of course to the fact that the raid at Celtic would have been the first action for many of the young men taking part. Men who were for the main part reinforcements joining the battalion a week or so before, making good the losses of Polygon Wood. That apart, Corporal E. Williams and Privates L. A. Green, C. C. Toll, D. A. Rhodes and T. Wilson were to be awarded the Military Medal for their efforts on that violent morning. All of them returned from the raid.

The report continues:

"Survivors who did return feel they were the equal man-to-man and we could all see from our front trench, in the early stages at least, what pluck and good leadership could do".

At 8 p.m. on the evening of the raid, the 9th October, the 10th Battalion were relieved by the 32nd Battalion, 5th Australian Division. They filed wearily out of the line via the Helles duckwalk track, back over Anzac Ridge so gloriously plucked from the enemy at the end of September, and across the canal bank to the area of Dominion Camp, a large hutted encampment west of Ypres near Poperinghe. There they would lick their wounds, collect their thoughts and mourn their colleagues, whilst reflecting on what might have been.

Lieutenant Frank J. Scott, 10th Battalion A.I.F. was the young commander of the raid on Celtic Wood on the 9th October 1917. He was mentioned in despatches but fell in the action and was never seen again. His name is commemorated on the Menin Gate Memorial to the Missing at Ypres, Belgium. He is pictured to the left here with his brother Lieutenant Cleve J. Scott who served in the same battalion under Lieutenant Colonel Wilder-Neligan. Lieutenant C. Scott was awarded the Military Cross for outstanding leadership during actions around Hollebeke on March 1st and 2nd 1918. He was killed in action whilst on patrol east of Merris on July 22nd 1918 during the battles around Hazebrouck and now lies at La Kreule British Cemetery approximately three kilometres from Hazebrouck.

Tony Traeger, with the help of Mr and Mrs Laurie Ronan of the Gawler Institute, Gawler, South Australia

A machine-gun post in trenches between Flinte Farm and Celtic on the eastern slopes of the Broodseinde Ridge, 5th October 1917. These troops are men of the 24th Battalion which was instrumental in capturing De Knoet Farm and the Broodseinde crossroads the day before. The slope down which men of the 10th Battalion attacked Celtic Wood on the 9th October can be seen on the sky-line.

Ted Smith

The southern edge of the slope that once was Celtic Wood. Men of the 10th Battalion attacked from the crest and down this slope into the wood on the morning of the 9th October 1917. Could the unexploded shell in the telegraph pole to the left of the photograph (see inset photo.) be a souvenir of the 5th Australian Divisional Artillery barrage?

Ted Smith

Lieutenant Colonel Wilder-Neligan's raid headquarters was sited in a dug-out exactly where the fence ends on the crest of this small slope south-west of the Broodseinde Ridge. His planning and orders for the raid on Celtic Wood were implemented from this remote but strangely nostalgic spot in a Flemish field.

8

THE CASUALTIES

"In the clash and bewilderment of actual fighting, in the rapid ruin and chaos and oblivion of the front line with its enormous process of annihilation, perhaps not many soldiers retained the confidence that the dead - themselves it might be to-morrow or the next instant - would at length obtain some lasting and distinct memorial."

Edmund Blunden.

THE CASUALTIES

THE question of casualties in battle and the variance of figures published have long perplexed researchers of the Great War. Casualty return detail has triggered many a debate among academics over the years and has clouded much after-comment concerning some of the greater campaigns. Various factions produce figures to make points or arguments whilst others explain that published returns cannot be valid and that true answers must be sought elsewhere.

In all the great battles and in smaller actions through to minor local operations and raids as was that at Celtic Wood, casualty returns are never detailed accurately enough to make the sense that one would like. In many cases the figures given never quite add up, or men who fell in a particular action are buried in cemeteries miles away from where the action took place. This is not due to any great plan of deception or confusion, but more likely the result of a system of record keeping that did not allow for the human factor when implemented at times of great trauma, stress and dramatic activity. Men who themselves were teetering at times on the edge of survival, working in abysmal dug-out conditions, under heavy shelling, possibly in immediate danger of themselves becoming one of the casualty figures they were recording, would endeavour to make these daily returns while no doubt feeling they had much more pressing problems to cope with. Any mistakes or omissions would be passed back to the more tranquil lifestyle at Brigade, Division or Corps headquarters where they would become 'cast in concrete' and compounded down the years. Is it any wonder that, seventy-odd years later, archives abound with totals, returns and 'facts' that do not always make the sense expected of them.

What of the casualties at Celtic Wood during that fateful encounter on the 9th October 1917? We know that eighty-five officers and other ranks took part in the raid on the wood, but what happened to them?

The Divisional report of the raid states :
"... our losses totalled forty officers and men."

The Brigade version states :
"... casualties were heavy taking into account size of the party - Forty all ranks."

The 10th Battalion History states :
"... about nineteen other ranks returned safely."

Lieutenant Colonel Wilder-Neligan's report states :
"... Lt. Scott and 2/Lt. Rae were killed. Lt. James and 2/Lt. Laurie came in slightly wounded, and 2/Lt.Wilsdon reported missing and not seen again ... very few wounded have passed through the dressing station ... I am only able to account for 14 unwounded members of the party" and hoped *"others might come in later"*

But did they? It is not documented so, nor were any prisoners or wounded recorded! No graves were found during the battlefield searches by the War Graves Commission in the post war years so, using the more detailed and positive report of Wilder-Neligan as a base for information, we know the fate of nineteen of the raiding party and are left with a figure of sixty-six men to account for.

We know that Lieutenant F. J. Scott and Second Lieutenant W. H. Wilsdon, D. C. M., mentioned in the report, are listed on the Menin Gate Memorial to the Missing at Ypres, together with twenty other ranks. All twenty-two are registered as having died on the 8th October - a certain error as it is beyond doubt that the raid took place on the 9th.

Add to these the two wounded officers, Lieutenant R. P. James and Lieutenant L. B. Laurie, and the fourteen unwounded men accounted for in the report and we arrive at a figure of thirty-eight. Second Lieutenant A. N. Rae, known to have died in the raid, together with Privates W. W. Charters and H. W. Barrow are buried near each other in Tyne Cot Military Cemetery with their deaths recorded as the 8th October - the same error compounded as for those listed on the Menin Gate Memorial. Another, Private E. L. Green, lies in Dochy Farm Military Cemetery and Lance Corporal C. A. Parker lies in the Hooge Crater Military Cemetery, again with the incorrect date of the 8th October as the registered date of their deaths. These five, whose bodies must have been discovered by members of the local farming community during the redevelopment of the area after the war, bring the total to forty-three officers and men, survivors and victims, who are known to have taken part in the raid. What of the remaining forty-two?

Tyne Cot Military Cemetery and those at Passchendaele, Lijssenthoek, the Buttes, Polygon Wood, Dochy Farm, Hooge Crater, Menin Road and Birr Cross Roads show no records of men of the 10th Battalion recorded as having died on the 8th October, other than those previously mentioned, or on the correct date of the 9th come to that. Sadly, there are many Australian soldiers in those cemeteries with headstone bearing the emotive inscription :
An Australian Soldier of the Great War Known unto God.

Could some of these be men of the fated 10th? If so, then

why are their names not recorded with their comrades, on the Menin Gate Memorial to the Missing? The Imperial War Graves Commission recognised that, to mark graves only, and to leave uncommemorated even one of the dead, would be a failure in duty, and it was decided to record, not only on paper, but in stone or bronze, the names of those who lay buried in unidentified graves, or under the battlefields. So what of the men of Celtic?

When researching official returns we find that the Battalion History lists the names of twenty-six who died on the 8th October. When compared with those on the Menin Gate Memorial, twenty-one accurately cross-reference, leaving only one, Private H. G. Mobbs, mentioned on the Memorial but not in the History. The remaining five tally with those buried in the Tyne Cot, Dochy Farm and Hooge Crater Military Cemeteries.

The History also records seven men as having died of wounds between the 8th (the recorded incorrect date of the raid) and the 15th October. These could have been casualties of the Celtic Wood raid, but then they could as well have been casualties of the German barrage of the 4th October battle which took its toll of the Battalion while in reserve in the China Wall area near Hell Fire Corner. Then again, they could have been the result of the move up to the line to relieve the 3rd Battalion on the 5th October. The 3rd Battalion History records this relief as :

"October 5th was a fairly quiet day, but towards dusk the German artillery renewed its fire, and the 10th Battalion had an unpleasant time moving up to take the place of the 3rd".

Further research shows two other ranks in the History who are recorded as dying *between* the 3rd and the 9th October. This gives an idea of the confusion and problems experienced in maintaining accurate records of men moving in large numbers before and after periods of battle.

It is also fair to assume that casualties would have been in-curred as a result of the many sporodic actions around Zonnebeke on the 9th October, so those seven men who died of wounds between the 8th and the 15th were not nec-essarily members of the raiding party who attacked Celtic Wood. Five of these casualties lie at Lijssenthoek Military Cemetry, one at Etaples and the other at Wimereux, both of these last two cemeteries being in France. It is very unlikely that the latter two, Privates E. F. Bleechmore and E. C. Fair-bairn, took part in the Celtic Wood action but quite possi-ble that the former five did. Lieutenant B. L. Laurie, who returned slightly wounded from the raid, died of wounds on the 27th April 1918 and is buried at Caestre Military Ceme-tery, France. Again, it is unlikely that his death was caused by wounds incurred at Celtic Wood. A total of forty-four men of the Battalion died of wounds from the 9th October 1917 to the 29th September 1918. Bearing in mind that the Battalion was in the line a further eight times during that period, with a casualty listing of six to seven hundred, then it is safe to assume that few of those who died did so of wounds received in the Celtic raid - but it is reasonable to assume that some did.

The History stated that :
"... about nineteen other ranks returned safely."
and the Wilder-Neligan raid report mentioned that :
"... very few wounded have passed through the dressing station"

It is most likely that the wounded would have passed through the Dressing Station at Birr Cross Roads and then continued on to the hospital camps at Lijssenthoek. The five men of the Battalion buried at this cemetery have their dates of death given as the 8th, 9th, 10th, 12th and 14th of October, and it would be acceptable to make the assump-

Footnote : A sad fact uncovered during research on 10th Batt. casualties. 25 year old Pte. Wille Campion died on 9th October during the Celtic Raid. His name is on the Menin Gate Memorial to the Missing at Ypres. His brother, 27 year old Pte. Gerald E. Campion died of wounds on 10th October, the day following the raid. He lays in Lijssenthoek Military cemetery. The brothers, in the same battalion and possibly casualties of the same raid, were natives of Minlaton, South Australia.

tion that they did die of wounds received during the Celtic raid - but we shall never know for sure!

So, taking into account these five men we assume to have died of wounds received during the raid, where does this mathematical exercise leave us? Add their names to those of the five buried in Tyne Cot, Dochy farm and Hooge Crater Military Cemeteries, the twenty-two named on the Memorial to the Missing at Ypres, the fourteen unwounded men and the two slightly wounded as mentioned in Wilder-Neligan's report and we reach the figure of forty-eight men accounted for. So what of the remaining thirty-seven other ranks of the raiding party? Are they missing from all records because of some form of clerical error made during a hectic and dangerous period? Did they return later during the day of the raid and continue about their soldierly duties without their presence being noted? Are they lying somewhere beneath the eastern slopes of the Broodseinde Ridge still waiting to be found? If so, why aren't their names recorded somewhere? The task would be easier if a list of the raiding party had been deposited in the Battalion archives. We would then have known for who we were looking, but it wasn't and we don't! So the question remains the same - where are their names recorded, or should it be why are their names *not* recorded?

Why did the Germans, such diligent and thorough record keepers, choose not to submit to the Red Cross a list of graves or of prisoners taken, or even to record the action. This would have thrown some light on the fate of those thirty-seven men. Did the Germans take any prisoners at all? Is there some other simple answer to the mystery of the whereabouts of those Australians at the time, or did they meet their fate in a more ominous manner? Did the Germans decide to take revenge on this group of men for the re-

Ted Smith

The Menin Gate Memorial to the Missing, Ypres, Belgium, 1990. The old gateway must hear the ghosts of countless legions as they enter the town each evening when the night is still, the traffic is stopped, and the Last Post hangs in the air.

10TH BN. AUSTRALIAN INFANTRY

LIEUTENANT
FORD R. P.
HERITAGE F. H. G. N.
MARTIN F W. S..M.M.
MILLS S. S..M. C.
SCOTT F. J.

SECOND LIEUT.
WILSDON W. H..D. C.M.

SERJEANT
COLE W.
CONNOCK E.
PAGE N. L.

CORPORAL
CHILD A.L.
HOLLIDAY W.
KELEY A. H.
LANCHESTER J. A.
McNAUGHTON E. F.
WILLIAMS R.W.

LANCE CORPORAL
CORY W. F. SERVED AS
         CORRIE A. F.
GREEN H.F.
REICH E.
STANTON E. R.B.

PRIVATE
ADAMS C.
ALLCHURCH G.
ALLEN E. R.
ARRING C. H.
BATES G. R..M.M.
BRADEY R. N.
BRYAN T.
BUCK A. H.
BUDER E. W.
CAMPION W. E.
CHARLESWORTH M.W.
CHRISTIAN W. L.
DACK H. R.
DALLY C. F.
DAVIES G. H. F.
DAVIS G. W.. M.M.
DEANS A.
DENING W. C.H.
DOIG J. J.
DULDIG O. R.
DUNCAN H. E.

PRIVATE
FERRES E. L.
FINCH W. G.
FOGGO R. A.
FREEMAN G.
GILL G. C.
GRAY F. T. R.
GRAY J.
HARRISON G. H.
HASS A. F.
JOHNS N. N.
KEEN A.W.
KNEALE R.R.
LANGLEY C. F. T.
LARKIN J. P.
LESTER F. J.
LLEWELYN D. L.
McMILLAN W.
MADLAND W. S.
MANGELSDORF W. H.
MILNES A. L.
MOBBS H. G.
MURPHY J. C.
NEALL A. E.
NEIL W.
NEWTON H.
OBORN H. M.
OLSTON F. A.
O'SULLIVAN E. A.
PENGEL A.
PHILLIPS A.V.
PICKEN J.
PRATT W. F.
PYBUS F. H.
ROBERTS J.
ROWNEY A. R.
SCHANTZ F.A.
SEIGERT G. W.
SHILLABEER A.W.
STRINGER H. E
THOMAS R.G.A.
THOMAS S.J.
TIDSWELL C. T. H.
TYLER G.
VIGAR O. V.
WARHURST F. K.
WARREN F. O.
WATERS M.S.
WELCH W. J.
WHITE W.A.
WHITFORD R.V.
WYE S.W.

Ted Smith

Names of men of the 10th Battalion A.I.F. on Panel 17, the Menin Gate Memorial to the Missing, Ypres, Belgium.

Tony Shepherd

The A.I.F. war memorial, Gawler, South Australia. The home town of
Lieutenant F. J. Scott, 10th Battalion. who led the raid on Celtic Wood.

The Chapel of Remembrance, Gawler, South Australia. A tribute to the men of Gawler who fell in the Great War. Lieutenant Scott and others of the 10th Battalion are honoured within.

cent humiliating and heavy defeats and then, in retrospect, cover-up the event by not recording the action, although there is no evidence to support such a theory, or at least there is none available?

There is yet another question concerning the raid that prompts similar thought. There are twenty-two men record-ed on the Menin Gate Memorial as having no known graves. They fell in a smallish well-contained piece of land which saw little or no action after the 9th October raid. Why then were no graves *or* bodies discovered in the area during the search in the immediate post war years? Were the bodies of those who fell collected by the Germans and buried in an unrecorded mass grave? Were the dead also to be made victims of an act of retribution and be denied a for-mal resting place alongside their comrades? We can only make assumptions and educated guesses from that which is recorded. What is sure however is that at dawn on the 9th October 1917, at a hitherto unknown wood east of the Broodseinde Ridge, the greater part of a band of Australians met their destiny and ended their days on this earth within the inexorable grinding of the teeth of war.

So the enigma of this casualty record rests with us and, if the 'Unknowns' are known only to God, then perhaps it prevails upon us to leave them in those rather splendid hands!

Is this then the definitive story of those who gave their lives so bravely in an abortive raid in a little known part of the Ypres Salient? Will we ever know the fate of those men from southern Australia? The circumstance of their deaths has at least dictated that the name of Celtic Wood lives on in our consciousness as a ghostly question mark, whereas more important actions and locations have long since van-ished from our memory.

Men of 10th Battalion named on panel No. 17 of the
Menin Gate Memorial with their deaths registered
incorrectly as the 8th October 1917.

Pte. Adams C.	Pte. Neall A. E.
Pte. Bates G. R. M. M.	Pte. Newton H.
Pte. Buck A. H.	Sgt. Page N. L.
Pte. Campion W. E.	Pte. Pybus F. H.
Sgt. Cole W.	Pte. Rowney A. R.
Pte. Davis G. W. M. M.	Lt. Scott F. J. *(Ment. in Desps.)*
Pte. Deans A.	Pte. Shillabeer A. W.
Pte. Doig J. J.	Pte. Thomas R. G. A.
Pte. Johns N. N.	Pte. Thomas S. J.
Pte. Mobbs H. G.	2/Lt. Wilsdon W. H. D. C. M.
Pte. Murphy J. C.	Pte. Ferguson R. A.
	(Addenda panel)

Men of the 10th Battalion buried with the incorrect date
of their deaths given as the 8th October 1917.

2/Lt. Rae A.N.	Tyne Cot Cemetery.
Pte. Barrow H. W.	Tyne Cot Cemetery.
Pte. Charters W.W.	Tyne Cot Cemetery.
Lce./Cpl. Parker C. A.	Hooge Crater Cemetery.
Pte. Green E. L.	Dochy Farm British Cemetery.

Men from the 10th Battalion who died of wounds and are
buried at Lijssenthoek British Military Cemetery

Pte. Campion G.G.	Died of wounds 10th October.
Pte. Leak R.A.	Died of wounds 9th October.
Pte. Patzel L.R.	Died of wounds 12th October.
Pte. Sample H.E.	Died of wounds 14th October.
Pte. Vawser W.H.	Died of wounds 8th October.

Lt. L. B. Laurie returned wounded from the raid. He died of wounds
in April 1918, but not necessarily of those incurred in the Celtic raid.
He lays in Caestre Military Cemetery, France.

Register references - The Menin Gate Memorial, Ypres, where men of the 10th Battalion are honoured.

Adams, Pte. Charles, 2780. 10th Bn. 8th Oct., 1917.
Age 35. Son of Charles Frederick and Jane Swain Adams, of Nungarin, W. Australia.

Bates, Pte. Glen Roy, 551, M. M. 10th Bn. 8th Oct., 1917.
Age 25. Son of Henry Frederick and Martha Bates of Hog Bay, Kangaroo Island, S. Australia.

Buck, Pte. Arthur Hart, 6966. 10th Bn. 8th Oct., 1917.
Age 26. Son of S. W. J. and Elizabeth Buck, of Kingscote, Kangaroo Island, South Australia.

Campion, Pte. Willie E., 2051. 10th Bn. 8th Oct., 1917.
Age 25. Son of Clara Campion, of Curramulka, South Australia, and the late Joseph Lenton Campion. Native of Minlaton, South Australia.

Cole, Serjt. William, 466. 10th Bn. 8th Oct., 1917.

Davis, Pte. Gilbert Walter, 5351, M. M. 10th Bn. 8th Oct., 1917.
Age 26. Son of Henry Archibald and Ruth Davis, of Riverton, South Australia

Deans, Pte. Adam, 3092. 10th Bn. 8th Oct., 1917.

Doig, Pte. James John, 3370. 10th Bn. 8th Oct., 1917. Age 37.
Youngest son of William Glen Doig and Mary Agness Doig, of 10, Drought St., Bendigo, Victoria. Native of Myer's Flat, Victoria.

Fergusson, Pte. Roy Albert, 4771. 10th Bn. 8th Oct., 1917.
Age 26. Son of Peter and Mary Ferguson, of Main Avenue, Frewville, South Australia.

Johns, Pte. Norman Nicholson, 5716. 10th Bn. 8th Oct., 1917.

Mobbs, Pte. Herbert George, 3649B. 10th Bn. 8th Oct., 1917.

Murphy, Pte. John Clare, 4530. 10th Bn. 8th Oct., 1917. Age 24. Son of Martin and Margaret Murphy. Native of Broken Hill, New South Wales.

Neall, Pte. Albert Edward, 2747B. 10th Bn. 8th Oct., 1917.

Newton, Pte. Herbert, 6805. 10th Bn. 8th Oct., 1917. Age 37. Son of Anne Newton, of 64, Cemetery Rd., Swinton, Manchester, England.

Page, Serjt. Norman Livingstone, 949. 10th Bn. 8th Oct., 1917. Age 28. Son of Elizabeth Anne Page, of Clara St., Murray Bridge, South Australia, and the late Stephen Page. Native of Wattle Dale, Aldgate, South Australia.

Pybus, Pte. Frederick Hagedorn, 150C. 10th Bn. 8th Oct., 1917. Age 26. Son of Frederick Henry and Elizabeth Jane Pybus. Native of Port Augusta, South Australia.

Rowney, Pte. Albert Ross, 2778B. 10th Bn. 8th Oct., 1917. Age 23. Son of Edward and Anne Rowney, of Cambelltown, South Australia.

Scott, Lt. Frank John. 10th Bn. Australian Inf. Mentioned in Despatches. 8th Oct., 1917. Age 23. Son of James and Felicia Rosina Scott, of "Frankleve," Church Hill, Gawler, South Australia. Native of Gawler, South Australia.

Shillabeer, Pte. Andrew William, 6821. 10th Bn. 8th Oct., 1917. Age 20. Son of Sam Millar Shillabeer and Sarah Isabella Shillabeer, of One Tree Hill, South Australia.

Thomas, Pte. Ronald George Albert, R/5763. 10th Bn. 8th Oct., 1917. Age 21. Son of William and Louisa M. Thomas, of Binnum, South Australia.

Thomas, Pte. Seymour Jacka, 6122. 10th Bn. 8th Oct., 1917. Son of John Henry and Elizabeth Anne Thomas, of Moonta, South Australia.

Wilsdon, 2nd Lt. Walter Harry, D.C.M. 10th Bn.
8th Oct., 1917. Age 24. Son of Charles William and Amy
Spottiswoode Wilsdon, of 2, Farrant St., Prospect, South Australia.
Native of Caltowie, S. Australia.

Register references - Military Cemeteries where men of the 10th Battalion who died in the Celtic raid are buried.

Tyne Cot Military Cemetery,
Passchendaele, Belgium.

Rae, 2nd Lt. Albert Norman. 10th Bn. Australian Inf.
Killed in action 8th Oct., 1917. Age 21. Son of Sophia Elizabeth
Rae, of West St., York, Kilkenny, South Australia, and the late
William Rae.
Plot XL. Row A. Grave 24.

Barrow, Pte. H. W., 2108. 10th Bn. Australian Inf. 8th Oct.,
1917.
Plot XXXVIII. Row B. Grave 23.

Charters, Pte. Walter William, 5673. 10th Bn. Australian Inf.
Killed in action 8th Oct., 1917. Age 29. Son of William Robert and
Mary Jane Charters, of 10, Divett Place, Adelaide, South Australia.
Plot XL. Row G. Grave 13.

Hooge Crater Militery Cemetery,
Zillebeke, Belgium.

Parker, Lce. Cpl. Charles Alexander, 1579. 10th Bn. Australian
Inf. Killed in action 8th Oct., 1917. Age 27. Son of Charles
Parker and of Christina West (formerly Parker), of Glanville Hotel,
Glanville, South Australia. Native of Port Adelaide.
Plot XIII. Row C. Grave 16.

Dochy Farm New British Cemetery,
Langemarck, Belgium.

Green, Pte Edward Louis, 2662B. 10th Bn. Australian Inf.
Killed in action 8th Oct., 1917. Age 25. Son of Louis and Mary
Anne Green, of Urailda, South Australia.
Plot VII. Row A. Grave 3.

Register references - Lissenthoek Military Cemetery where men of the 10th Battalion who died of wounds assumed to have been incurred in the Celtic raid are buried.

Campion, Pte. Gerald Gordon, 1920. 10th Bn. Australian Inf. Died of wounds 10th Oct., 1917. Age 27. Son of Clara and the late Joseph Lenton Campion, of Curramulka, South Australia. Native of Minlaton, South Australia.
Plot XXI. Row D. Grave 19A.

Leak, Pte. Reginald Arthur, 6779. 10th Bn. Australian Inf. Died of wounds 9th Oct., 1917. Son of Henry Leak, husband of Edith Leak, of Dudley St., Semaphore, South Australia. Native of Goodwood, South Australia.
Plot XXI. Row B. Grave 12A.

Patzel, Pte. Lawrence Ralph, 6810. 10th Bn. Australian Inf. Died of wounds 12 Oct., 1917. Age 25. Son of Mr. and Mrs. G. A. Patzel, of Mount Gambier, South Australia.
Plot XX. Row J. Grave 3A.

Sample, Pte. Henry Ewert, 1326. 10th Bn. Australian Inf. Died of wounds 14th Oct., 1917.
Plot XXI. Row C. Grave 21.

Vawser, Pte. William Herbert, 6844. 10th Bn. Australian Inf. Died of wounds 8th Oct., 1917.
Plot XXI. Row D. Grave3A.

Register reference - Caestre Military Cemetery, France, where Lt. Laurie, wounded in the Celtic raid, is buried.

Laurie, Lt. Leonard Buxton. 10th Bn. Australian Inf. Died of wounds 27th April., 1918. Son of John Buxton Laurie and Ada Laurie, of Salisbury, South Australia.
Plot I. Row B. Grave 18.

The foregoing register entries have been reproduced with the kind permission of the Commonwealth War Graves Commission, Maidenhead, Berkshire.

9

CONCLUSION

"There is only one thing real in life, and that is eternity. War remains at best a nauseous blasphemy "

Hugh Quigley.

CONCLUSION

T HERE was no substantial list of enemy losses recorded after the Celtic Wood operation. After all, who on the Australian side had been able to stay in the fight long enough to compile such a profit and loss account? We already know that the Germans, as meticulous as they were in all matters concerning their activities in the war, did not list any such detail, having omitted to document the raid at all.

The majority of the survivors who did return, did so early in the day, or came back that night having lain out in the safety of a shell hole. None was able to describe the closing stages of this brutal encounter when Lieutenant Scott's gallant little band was finally destroyed at the southern edge of the wood.

One can speculate endlessly as to what went wrong without reaching any firm conclusion. Would it be safe to assume that the Australian perception of the German response was a little optimistic? Did they really expect to strike him twice within thirty-six hours at the same sensitive spot and not exact some violent response? Did the raiders, perhaps made confident by the early success, get sucked too deep into the wood and the resultant tragedy?

Might it not have been more prudent, it always is in retrospect, to have adhered rigidly to the raid plan, which was to hit the enemy hard into expecting a larger attack. Then, when he was off-balance and confused, the raiders would create a little mayhem, destroying dug-outs and gun-pits, picking up a few dazed prisoners and finally returning to the safety of their lines before the Germans could recover, and in the knowledge of a job well done. In the case of the Celtic raiders, once they were at the point of no return in the wood and the sudden violent enemy barrage descended to cut off their escape route, their fate was sealed and there could only be one logical ending.

Why the raid was conceived at only company strength if the intention was to delude the enemy is a mystery. The official Australian historian, C. E. W. Bean, is quite vague about this and the official papers do not disclose why, and at what level, the decision was taken. Probably it was made at divisional level. Most of the available artillery was obviously going to be needed to support II Anzac's effort to the north. This led to the alleged thin barrage during the Celtic demonstration.

The real question to be asked of course, is whether the raid was worth attempting - and the answer must be a resounding *No!* A few light guns and a depleted infantry company were unlikely to have fooled the Germans for long. The same effect could have been achieved by an artillery shoot in strength alone, without risking the lives of eighty-five first class infantrymen. Even after all these years one can only feel sympathy for Lieutenant Scott and his raiding party.

Did the Germans, for once in a position to repay the Australians in some measure, exact some terrible retribution on all those trapped in Celtic Wood? We shall never really know. Perhaps somewhere in Germany an ageing veteran playing out his final years might recall his part in the defence of a little wood east of Broodseinde in October 1917?

We can stand today on that gentle slope above the site of where Celtic Wood once stood and, in the evening stillness, try to reconcile the pastoral scene before us with the violent events of so many years ago and hope and trust that the young Australians, who travelled half the world from their homes under the Southern Cross to find their last resting place at this spot, will not be forgotten, but honoured and remembered.

Few warrior graves mark their passing this way, only some of their names, carved with pride on the stone panels of the Menin Gate, together with six headstones in Tyne Cot, Dochy Farm, Hooge Crater and Caestre British Military Cemeteries remain with us today.

Australia is a young nation, although her roll of military honours belies the fact. In saying that, at what better place could be heard more proudly the ghostly strains of *Advance Australia Fair* than on the ridge of Broodseinde above where once stood the little wood known as Celtic.

"Unknown! Ah, no! thy name still lives,
For one has seen thee fall,
And marked the sacrifice thus made,
The debt of love so nobly paid,
Faithful to Freedom's call."

"Unknown, and yet .... well known."

Lieutenant Wilfred Halliday, Poet.
7th Battalion, West Yorks Regiment.
Killed in action, Ypres 1917.

10

REFLECTIONS

"This ground will be forever haunted by that noble youth of ours, by those muddy men in steel hats, by the surge of transport and guns, by the ghosts of a great army of youth, so cheery even on the edge of abominable ordeal, so valiant in the face of death itself, so patient in suffering, so stubborn in endurance, so simple and splendid by the faith that was in them and never told."

Sir Philip Gibbs. K.B.E.

REFLECTIONS

A NYONE visiting the Broodseinde area today can walk or drive down the gentle slopes that descend the eastern ridge to the farm buildings that stand near the site of the original Celtic Wood. Regrettably the Belgians, with their progressive ribbon development, have built along the crest obscuring part of the view, but the expanse of ridge covered in the raid by the 10th Battalion, now open farm land, can still be seen in many places. Where the ground has been farmed and modern builders prevented from encroachment, a small group of trees extending east along the minor road towards the Keiburg Spur indicates part of the area that once formed Celtic Wood.

It was down this road at the south-east end of the ridge, which also leads to the little hamlet of Waterdamhoek, that the local German commanders hurried their emergency reserve troops to help overpower and quell the smaller Australian party led by Lieutenant Scott, then trapped within the confines of the wood. It was also down this road that a dishevelled Major Wegehaupt, panic stricken after the brutal fighting around the command bunker in the crater on the ridge top, ran to give the grave news to garrison headquarters that the 4th October battle was becoming, for them, a major disaster on their immediate front.

Another location to stand and ponder the fate of Lieuten-

ant Scott and his men is on the smaller track north of the
road to the Keiburg.   Here, just where the track ends its
sweep in an angled bend to the left, is the precise spot
where the fire-pits crossed the track line.   It was these
trenches that housed D Company. (See Battle Map facing
page 40).   Just before the raid commenced C Company
joined D Company in these trenches and eventually left
them to move warily down the misty slope in a south-
easterly direction to meet what we now know was their fate,
with the greater part of them never to return.   Directly the
raid commenced D Company also left these trenches and
took up their support position for the raid in trenches to the
direct west of the wood, now part identifiable by the farm
and outbuildings standing on the old trench line.   This farm
stands on the site of the original Celtic Farm which formed
part of the German defences during 1917.

Anyone with imagination and sensivity can perceive this
area to be an emotive section of the old Salient front to visit, to read about and to ponder over trench maps in a bid to
make sense of it all, and to attempt to relate to the various
points and events which surrounded the raid on Celtic
Wood

Back along the western slope of the ridge, and not too far
distant from these old trench lines, sits a large, prosperous
farming complex on a knoll just below the peaceful, rural
cross roads of Broodseinde - in October 1917 the notorious
Broodseinde Cross Roads so fiercely fought for amid the
graves of a large German military cemetery that once
spanned them.   This farm is sited on the original De Knoet
farm, and retains that name today.   Up to October 1917 it
commanded a superior view back across Zonnebeke and Polygon Wood to Ypres itself.   A major German strong-point,
safe and secure for them, and a menacing obstacle to any of

the allied forces who chose to attempt to tread this area of
German superiority.   Or so they, the Germans, thought.
The Australian 2nd Division thought otherwise and, on the
4th October 1917, they made their presence known with
speed and decisiveness by sweeping aside the horrors that
De Knoet farm represented and making it their own.

Lower down the slope in the valley below, nestling aside
the little track running past the Zonnebeke Lake and
Château is another farm on the site of its predecessor, long
since gone. Known in the war years as Retaliation Farm it,
and its surrounding area, was another important German
strongpoint in their defensive line.   Here was witnessed
some of the most brutal close combat and bayonet fighting
of the early stages of the 4th October battle. Today it wears
a mantle of peaceful calm which sorely belies its violent
past.

Back on the ridge-top road a junction leads to a small
track winding in a north-easterly direction from the Celtic
area, past Cyclops Farm and on to Flinte Farm and its ad-
joining Flinte Copse. Both farms were part of the extremely
well organised German defence line and the copse itself was
one of many hereabouts utilised so skilfully on the eastern
side of the ridge following the collapse of the main defences
on the western slopes and ridge top. Evidence of concrete
works can still be seen near the farm and copse areas. A little stream feeding quietly into the site of the copse was identified by a local farmer as being a water supply used, and
made use of, by the "Allemand" occupiers. Part of what is
left of the long tongue of Flinte Copse is recognisable today
when compared with the maps of the time - only then it was
reinforced and manned by resolute defenders whose main
aim was to make it dangerous for any Australians or British
who dared venture down to this section of the ridge.

A fine view of the high ground around Passchendaele village and church to the north-west brings everything into perspective and spells out more adequately than any words can tell as to just how important this whole area was to the German Army, and what the Australians had achieved by taking the Broodseinde Ridge.

If their brief had been to continue to advance following the major successes on the 4th October, then who knows what might have transpired? The German defenders at Passchendaele would most certainly have seen the advance developing below them as a very serious threat to their overall position. Being alarmed and wary of a possible outflanking and enveloping move by an ebullient foe, they might have considered it sound, prudent and an effective military tactic, to have relinquished the village and its ridge. Thus the battle would have closed down for the winter, six weeks before it actually did! Wishful military thinking perhaps? Who can tell? Such are the improbables in retrospect which are so intriguing in situations such as these.

To visit this area is a pilgrimage in the fullest sense of the term, and one is often reduced to an inner sense of deep pride mingled with sadness when attempting to come to terms with the momentous events that have taken place on the very land which now supports a friendly and industrious farming community. It is sometimes difficult to accept the total unawareness of the local Belgians to the tragedies that took place over the ground where they build their homes, spend their workdays and leisure time and bring up their families. Like their compatriots all over this part of Belgium they do this on ground which has soaked up the blood of so many young men from so many countries and so many walks of life.

This is progress and the way of the world no doubt and

better it be that they stay unaware and, hopefully, the flat lands of Flanders will never again experience the death and destruction visited upon them during those grim but strangely noble years from 1914 to 1918. Grim that such a vast potential of manhood was so tragically lost to their families, their country and to us all. Noble in a manner that man's loyalty to values, to courage and to his humanity for his fellows, shone like a beam through all these terrors to enrich those who follow them over the years.

On a thoughtful walk back from Flinte Copse to the site of Celtic Wood, a colleague mused in sombre mood:- *"I wonder what the German ration and carrying parties who passed along here just before dawn on the 9th October, 1917 were thinking ? Did the flares over the ridge worry them? Did they wonder if the Australians were coming yet again?*

Well, yes, they were coming - and they did come! Most of them never left and are still here. Let's hope that, wherever they are, they sometimes hear the sound of the nightly ritual played out in their honour at the Menin Gate, Ypres.

As the clear, pure notes of the Last Post linger hauntingly on the still evening air - may they all rest in peace.

Ypres, November 11th, 11 a.m.

When the bugles sound again this day
We shall hear
And come, though far away,
To answer yet again Reveille's call;
Though memories make this meeting hard to bear
Some brief and precious minutes we can spare
To greet you,
For this was our world too,
So full of hopes and dreams unborn,
So soon to vanish with Death's early dawn;
We come to say again -
Call us with bugles, not with guns,
So shall we know our sacrifice was not in vain,
So 'till all battles cease and the Earth's at peace
We will remember ... We will remember ...
We will remember ...

Pat Freeman
1989

SERGEANT COMBES D.C.M.
ZOUAVE WOOD 4th OCTOBER 1917.
(Reference page 12)

I T had already been noted by Australian and British observers that the German artillery, which had saturated
the luckless infantry laying out on the wet ground in front
of their own lines all along the base of the ridge from Polygon Wood to the Tokio Spur, had caused a great deal of
concern There was apprehension as the weight of the shell-
fire intensified and casualties mounted at such a critical
point just prior to the attack to be launched by the Anzac
Corps on the Broodseinde Ridge.

An enemy counter-attack at this juncture had not been
anticipated. It was unnerving for the ridge watchers to even
remotely contemplate that the offensive would be contested
strongly by a rejuvenated enemy, supposedly on his knees,
after a string of recent reverses.

All down the line enemy guns searched and probed in an
attempt to destroy the known approach tracks which could
be utilised by the British. Every copse or farm building still
standing, every sunken road or fold and dip in the ground
which could house troops or hide gun batteries was battered
and received its fair ration of death and destruction sent
over with the compliments of the 'House of Krupps'!

The roads and tracks through the once wooded glades of

85

Polygon and Glencorse Woods and the military road through the confines of Château Wood at Bellewaarde were death traps for the unwary as the barrage heralding the Germans' own counter-measure reached a crescendo! A large natural basin of ground in front of Hooge Château and lake known as Dead Man's Bottom, a place known for the concentrating of men, became a vortex of fire before the ranges were lifted slightly to play the last vestiges of hate through Railway Wood to end up on the Menin Road at Hell Fire Corner, almost at the gates of Ypres itself!

It was close to Hell Fire Corner at the extreme range of the German retribution that, by one of wars' ironies, their fire would briefly involve the men of the 10th Battalion A.I.F. who were part of 3rd Brigade Reserves housed around Halfway House, a large ruined farm with spacious cellars sited close to the village of Zillebeke. Tragic, isolated incidents were being played out all along the line, and one such cameo was about to be enacted here. The young men of the Battalion, most of whom had not seen any major action, having just recently joined the unit as reinforcements following the Polygon Wood battles of September, were still several days away from their own date with destiny at Celtic Wood, an appointment which would affect so many of their lives. Those in C Company must have eyed their young commander, Lieutenant Scott, rather nervously as they hunched in the shelters and dug-outs along their position at China Wall, a large well-appointed breastwork-come-communication trench which snaked-in at an angle from just west of Hell Fire Corner towards Halfway House. They must have blinked and thought of home as they heard the crunch and smash of heavy calibre shells exploding around them as the guns searched with intent to inflict maximum damage. Lieutenant Scott, an experienced officer, might have viewed his young charges with concern as the perspiration gathered on furrowed brows, and tension grew as they bunched together in cramped quarters. Perhaps his own thoughts ranged back fleetingly to happier, more carefree days spent at home in Gawler, South Australia, but his experience told him there was a job to be done and, for the moment, that was to keep his men safe and calm, and to await any orders to move up the line if needed to support the general attack. The continuous enemy fire by its very nature was causing sporadic casualties throughout the narrow brigade area, and even though records today can never prove the point, it is probably safe to assume that the few 10th Battalion fatalities of the 4th October, 1917 found in the local British cemeteries probably stem from the pounding received hereabouts. The Australians, hemmed into this small concentrated area, knew they could hardly be the specific target for the German guns, but also, they could have hardly failed to notice that several British artillery units were stationed in and around the ridge leading up to the battered hamlet of Hooge and the large natural valley suitable for the siting of heavy guns that lay between Château Wood and Sanctuary Wood. From the sprawling mass of the latter, a small section of woodland named Zouave Wood could be seen, so called from more tranquil days when it safely housed French Colonial troops. It was now a smouldering and blackened mass of ruined trees and bushes which currently housed a battery of heavy British guns and their sweating teams preparing to support the general corps attack by Australian infantry on the Broodseinde Ridge several kilometers ahead to the east. This unit, the 17th Heavy Battery, Royal Garrison Artillery, had just come up after a spell stationed on the Comines canal at the Spoilbank. The Battery, with its four sections of heavy guns had a strength of over two hundred horses and one hundred and sixty men under the command of Major G. G. Walker and his second in command, Captain W. Fenn. The gun teams, command staff and the Australian soldiers in shelters nearby held their breath in trepidation as the ranging enemy fire came nearer.

The Battery War Diary for dawn on the 4th October 1917 details clearly what happened next:

"Our bombardment opened at 6 a.m. - but during the preparation for this at 5.50 a.m. enemy shelled battery position causing heavy casualties as follows:- Gunner Gimblett (killed). Gunner Calvert (wounded - but died later in day). Sgt Combes, Gunners Tierney, Dunbar, White and Jolley all wounded and on to hospital. Battery and dugouts heavily shelled during the afternoon".

One of the Battery stalwarts at this critical time was Sergeant Harry Combes, a thirty-two year old from Chichester, Sussex. Harry was a battery sergeant of the old school, a professional soldier with years of service behind him, so typical of the British Army non-commissioned officer of the time - the type of soldier who had made the army of the 1914 period such a formidable force for the German Imperial Army to contend with.

Sergeant Combes now brought his experience to bear as he stood his ground, steadied the men under his command and, as the smoke cleared, saw them through those vital dangerous moments following such a tragic calamity. Although stunned and wounded himself, he ensured the rest of the Battery engaged the unseen enemy gunners at Broodseinde before removing his wounded men to hospital or for much needed attention via the Dressing Station close by at Birr Cross Roads on the Menin Road.

For his conduct and example on this day Sergeant Harry

Sergeant Harry Combes D.C.M., Royal Garrison Artillery. His Distinguished Conduct Medal was awarded for gallantry near Zouave Wood, Ypres, Belgium, at dawn on the 4th October 1917. Sergeant Combes died in 1930. (Post war photograph taken in 1925).

Combes would be recommended for a well-earned Distinguished Conduct Medal, the citation of which appeared in the London Gazette of January 1918 :

282298 Sjt. II. Combes, R.G.A. (Chichester).
For conspicuous gallantry and devotion to duty in keeping his gun in action under heavy fire of every description. One gun of his section was put out of action, and the remaining sub-sections were forced to withdraw to cover. He, however, stood fearlessly in the open in the rear of his gun and kept it in action against a hostile battery, thus setting a splendid example of pluck and determination to all ranks at a critical time.

After 6 a.m. when the British barrage had completely enveloped the German Broodseinde positions, and the Australian infantry had begun to secure the ridge, the enemy counter fire began to slacken-off and the smoke and flame lifted and cleared from the Menin Road, Hell Fire Corner and the China Wall area. The gunners of the 17th Heavy Battery began to clear up their shattered gun-site and, together with the men of the 10th Battalion, emerged into the fresher air to lick their lips, and to give thanks to whoever they considered responsible for their escape from the hellish German barrage. Lieutenant Scott and his young soldiers had been given a reprieve - but for how long? They would have to make the most of the extra time allowed them, for in a hundred and twenty hours exactly, the ruined stumps of Celtic Wood would offer a much more sombre challenge for so many of them. It is fervently hoped it would come to pass that, in the immortal words of the poet Wilfred Owen :
"Some say God caught them even before they fell".
As for the hero of this little episode, Harry Combes, his thoughts would have been on many things as he moved

rearward to receive some much needed medical attention. This well experienced, responsible and caring non-commissioned officer would view the morning's events with mixed emotions without knowing he was on his way to an award for gallantry.

He had endured the painful loss of two friends in action and several others badly injured. It was a morning that would live in his memory for the rest of his life!

The 17th Heavy Battery stayed in the Ypres Salient in a support gunnery role until the 28th October 1917 when it was transferred to First Army Reserve Corps near Bethune, northern France. Captain Fenn was the new commander when this transfer took place.

Sergeant Harry Combes survived the war to return home to his family in England, but sadly passed away in 1930.

Of his two colleagues who fell so gallantly during the shelling of the Battery area on the 4th October at Zouave Wood, Gunner Gimblett lies in The Huts British Military Cemetery at Dickebusch, and Gunner Calvert in the Menin Road British Military Cemetery near Hell Fire Corner.

"Cloth Hall. Ypres". From a lithograph by Daryl Lindsay.

MAJOR PAGE - A CLOSE SHAVE
(Reference page 15)

A T Zonnebeke the Australian 2nd Division attackers flowed forward like an irresistible flood, running-out over the Tokio Spur just south of the village and either side of the ruined village church, château, château lake and the small, dense woodland which embraced all these features.

Men from the 21st Battalion quickly eliminated hostile machine-guns around the ruins of the church and château before too many problems were caused for the main force of attackers. They then headed, with their fellow 24th Battalion from 6th Brigade, eastwards toward the ominous mass of De Knoet Farm perched threateningly on its knoll below the Broodseinde crossroads. The defences here were expected to cause a major obstacle to the objective of gaining the ridge crest. Attacks with hand-bombs and bayonets by the Australians quickly secured this farm and it was here that the entrenched enemy experienced the frightening exhibition of bravery shown by Private W. E. Oliver who calmly walked amongst them firing his Lewis machine-gun from the hip ... and survived!

The attacking brigades just south of the château had to pass round different sides of the infamous Zonnebeke lake, a bleak waterhole two hundred yards long by one hundred wide and now a soggy morass of mud, swamp and water. In order to maintain connection with each other, a detached platoon from the 22nd Battalion of 6th Brigade south of the lake was to make contact with the 25th Battalion of 7th Brigade north of the lake while a flank platoon of the 25th would pass to the south.

Major H. Page of the 25th, moving forward with his men south of the lake, mistook a number of figures in the mist ahead of him for Australians but, on walking over to join them, he found to his dismay that they were in fact German infantry from the 212th Regiment moving forward to launch an enemy attack. He was quickly overpowered and made prisoner and one of his captors tried to take his revolver which was attached to his wrist. Some desultory shelling was still taking place around this area of the lake and a British shell falling uncomfortably close caused everyone, Australians and Germans alike, to scatter. Quickly recovering and retaining some composure, Major Page fired his revolver at the enemy several times and was able to duck into the mist making good his escape back to his battalion comrades.

The result of this dramatic little episode must have been disappointing for the Germans concerned because a recent command offered rewards and leave to those troops who brought in a prisoner - and the higher the rank of the prisoner the higher the rewards. Major Page was obviously seen as a nice bonus during a not very pleasant period for those unfortunate German soldiers.

Major Page came through the battles for the Ridge and went on to command the 25th Battalion during 1918. He was severely wounded in the action at Mont St. Quentin near Peronne in September of that year. He returned to Australia in June 1919.

THE CRATER SITE TODAY
(Reference page 18)

HALF-WAY along the pavé road that followed the crest of the ridge south from Passchendaele to Becelaere, the road took a severe swerve to pass around a large crater at the edge of the ridge. This crater had presumably been blown by an ammunition dump explosion earlier in the war. Quick to perceive its tactical importance and its valuable field of fire and observation, the Germans constructed a large pill-box within it to act as a headquarter base. At the time of the Australian attack on the Broodseinde Ridge of the 4th October 1917, it housed the staff of the forward battalions of the I/5th Foot Guards and the II/212th Infantry Regiment.

From here the Germans were able to bring all manner of fire to bear on any luckless infantry bold enough to debouch from Polygon Wood making for the ridge. Or so they thought! The Australians had been very successful around this feature following the bravery of Captain H. Annear of the 6th Battalion. It was from here that, after the collapse of the defences, Major Wegehaupt, commander of the 1st Battalion, 5th Foot Guards, managed to escape down the Waterdamhoek road on the reverse slope of the ridge to the headquarters of the support battalion at Celtic Wood. He arrived about 7 a.m. and reported that both the previously

mentioned battalions had been overrun. The crater was situated approximately four hundred metres south of where the
British 7th Division memorial stands today and maps of the
time show how the crest road swerved in a semi-circle
around its outline. To stand at the site of the crater today
enables one to see better than any words can describe the
quite extraordinary observation advantage the Germans en-
joyed, both westward towards Ypres and eastward towards
the Keiburg Spur and Roulers.

There are no traces of either the crater or the pill-box to
be found today for the modern researcher to reflect upon.
In the post war years the crater was filled-in and the pill-box
dismantled. During the development of the area, when the
road was straightened and houses built, the remains of the
pill-box were used as part of the footings of one of the road-
side dwellings.

A house practically on the site is owned by a friendly retired couple who were kind enough to invite a colleague and
myself into their home during our search for evidence of the
crater's position. We learnt from them that part of the front
yard area of the house next door was built on top of the remains of the pill-box - and that we were actually sitting,
drinking coffee and talking, at a table on the edge of where
that infamous crater was. The neighbouring house is owned
by this couple's son and daughter-in-law and, with typical
Belgian hospitality, we were introduced to them. They added to our findings by explaining that, during the excavations
to prepare the footings of the house, the builders were clearing loose soil to a depth of about nine feet alongside the
pill-box and bringing up German equipment, clothing and
other artefacts of war.

Ted Smith

Halfway House. The 10th Battalion headquarters during the Battle of the Broodseinde Ridge. photographed from China Wall Military Cemetery. Hooge Crater Military Cemetery can be seen in the distance to the left of the farm. The battery of Sergeant Combes D.S.O would have been sited on the slopes seen behind Hooge Crater cemetery during the German barrage of 4th October 1917. Zoauve Wood was originally sited in the right middle distance in front of the slope of the Hooge Ridge

The crater and command pill-box which was the centre of the fierce resistance experienced by the Australians in the battle for the Broodseinde Ridge on the 4th October 1917. Captain Annear and Major Taylor of the 6th Battalion lost their lives during and just after the action which resulted in the capture of this pill-box. Major Wegehaupt escaped from here and ran to Celtic Wood to break the news of the disaster to his colleagues.

Ted Smith

The command pill-box and crater site as it looks today, 1990. While preparing the foundations for the house on the right the builders were digging down to a depth of 9 feet alongside the pill-box and bringing up various artefacts of war in the process. Captain H. N. Annear and Major C. H. Taylor of the 6th Battalion were killed in this area during the fighting to capture the pill-box.

IWM Q.45461

What remained of Zonnebeke Church, October 1917. This was Zonnebeke Church and lake after three years of modern warfare. Major Page had his 'close shave' just south of this lake.

Zonnebeke Church and lake, October 1990.

Ted Smith

Ted Smith

Remi Farm as seen from within the Lijssenthoek (Remi Sidings) British Military Cemetery. 5 men of the 10th Battalion who died of wounds assumed to have been inflicted during the Celtic Wood raid are buried here as is Captain Annear who died so valiantly while attacking the command post in the crest-top crater.

Ted Smith

Remi Sidings and the road built atop the old railway embankment. Now a major road to the old rail link where thousands of wounded men were transported to the hospitals and the coast. The photograph is looking towards the town of Steenvoorde and the French frontier.

Ted Smith

The China Wall area with Hell Fire Corner and the Menin Road in the distance. This area housed the men of the 10th Battalion while in reserve during the 4th October attacks. The chapel at the village of Hooge is at the distant right of the photograph.

CAPTAIN H. N. ANNEAR
REMI SIDINGS, LIJSSENTHOEK
(Reference page 18)

CAPTAIN Harry Annear was a company commander in the 6th Battalion Australian Infantry when they advanced under heavy fire up the Broodseinde Ridge on the morning of the 4th October 1917. A furious curtain of fire and a most resolute resistance centred around the crater and the pill-boxes in its vicinity, sited on the western edge of the main road which ran along the crest-line of the ridge. The 6th Battalion battle-plan called for them to eliminate the defence of the crater to ensure the minimum of delay to the main advance.

As the Australians edged-in over open sights, the main resistance seemed to be coming from the area of the crater itself and the numerous little pill-box forts close to it - all spitting-out a venomous fire. This fire, coupled with that of the machine-guns manned by elite squads at the crater, took a very heavy toll of the main attackers as they advanced further to the north against Broodseinde itself. Something had to be done! Someone had to make a move! Outflanking parties from the 6th Battalion under the command of Major Taylor and Captain Annear rushed the crater from several directions. For a few vital moments it was mayhem but then Captain Annear was seen walking coolly around the brim of the crater, stepping over wire, bodies and other debris and shooting down at the enemy with his revolver while they threw bombs at him. Almost immediately he was mortally wounded.

The crater and pill-box were captured and, as Major Taylor stood up at the side of the crater to organise the survivors, he was shot and killed - a severe loss to the 6th Battalion and the 2nd Brigade. He was buried near to the crater's edge during the furious fighting and a marker was placed accordingly. His grave could not be located after the battle and his name is honoured on the Menin Gate Memorial to the Missing at Ypres.

Later in the day when the immediate fighting had subsided, Captain Annear was taken back to the brigade casualty Collecting Post near Hooge and then transported by ambulance to the main hospitals sited around Remi Sidings, Lijssenthoek just south of Poperinghe. The delay in his receiving attention and the shock caused by his wounds took their toll and he died the next day, the 5th October 1917.

This gallant twenty-three year old soldier now lies at rest in the main British Military Cemetery at Lijssenthoek, the second largest war cemetery after Tyne Cot. It was set-up after the Armistice on the site of the old Remi Sidings, the main railhead for casualties being transported out of the battle areas to the hospitals and rest centres back on the coast around Boulogne.

Captain H. N. Annear was born in Yapeen, Victoria on the 22nd May 1894. He worked in the shoe trade as a last maker before commencing his military service.

The Germans often raided the Remi Sidings area at night and were fiercely criticised because of the concentration of hospitals sited there. They in turn defended their actions by accusing the British of using the rail link to bring in men and supplies, and of having several fighter squadrons based around Poperinghe and Proven - which of course was the truth!

Today Remi Sidings is a cluster of peaceful fields with nothing more important than the growing of hops as its principle activity. Remi *Hoeve*, or farm house, is still there with suspicious signs of English military-style architecture amongst its outbuildings. The railway no longer exists but the long, straight road now built in its place is supported by the old railway embankment.

Remi Sidings, or Lijssenthoek Military Cemetery, itself on the other side of the farm, can be seen through the farm buildings and surrounding trees from the roadway. It takes very little imagination to picture and compare the solemn events of the dead being buried in that cemetery sited on one side of the farm complex, with the happier, but nevertheless sad activity on the other, where the wounded were being entrained for transportation back to the caring safety of the coastal hospitals and, for some, maybe even Blighty.

"Full Marching Order". From a Lithograph by Daryl Lindsay.

AUSTRALIAN V.C.'S
SEPTEMBER - OCTOBER 1917
(Reference page 37)

THE 10th Battalion, 1st Australian Division took part in the opening assault in the Battle of the Menin Road, Third Ypres, on the 20th September 1917. Their objective, the vast and menacing expanse of Polygon Wood. This infamous wood represented a fortress in the centre of the German line, filled with pill-boxes and networked with wire protected trench lines. One of the first Victoria Crosses awarded to the 10th Battalion was won by Private Reginald R. Inwood for his sterling work of the 21st and 22nd September during this battle. On the night of the 21st he was one of a party who undertook a scouting operation five-hundred yards ahead of the Australian front line to locate and identify enemy positions and infantry regiments around the "Butte" at the north-eastern edge of the wood. Early the next morning, the 22nd September, he detected a potentially dangerous machine-gun position and, with an unnamed comrade, moved forward, bombed it, killed a number of the enemy, captured the gun and took a prisoner, whom he made carry the gun back to Australian lines, thus eliminating a dangerous obstacle to the Australian advance.

Private Inwood, born in Renmark, survived the war and died in Adelaide at seventy-one years of age on the 23rd Oct. 1971.

October 1917 was to prove to be a most busy period for the Australian Corps and a time when trained observers had seen them as most efficient and effective. They had obviously shrugged off the disasters of Fromelles and Pozières of the previous year as well as the severe bruising they had experienced at Bullecourt in April and May of 1917. Now, since the middle of September, their hammer-blows to capture Polygon Wood and the Broodseinde Ridge had severely embarrassed the enemy's battle plans to defend the high ground around Passchendaele. The Anzac battalions could only have continued with their successes and added to their reputation and prowess had they not been hampered and eventually halted by the horrendous weather conditions.

Following the attack of the 9th October and the subsidiary operation at Celtic Wood, they were still very active right up to the middle of the month, clinging desperately to the toe-hold they occupied on the highest part of the Passchendaele Ridge, within sight of the village itself. From the 12th of the month they were heavily engaged, as II Anzac Corps battled furiously against a tough and resilient foe. They were eventually relieved by the incoming Canadian Corps who would go on to secure the crest and the village of Passchendaele. The weather continued to cause tremendous problems right up to the period when the fighting subsided around the 10th November.

The ominous collection of pill-boxes around Tyne Cot had fallen in the advance of the 4th October and it was during this operation, and that around the two neighbouring fortified farm strongpoints of Hamburg and Beecham, that twenty-nine year old Sergeant Lewis McGee of the 40th Battalion won his Victoria Cross. He had already achieved a fine war record fighting with distinction at Bullecourt in April of that year. Now his bravery and excellent leadership qualities served him well as the obstacles of pill-boxes and machine-gun nests were gradually eliminated. He was recommended for a battlefield commission and the Victoria Cross. This gallant soldier would never know of these honours as he was killed by machine-gun fire a few days later on the 12th October while leading his men in a probe near Augustus Wood, a little further up the ridge, .

Lewis McGee was born in Ross, Tasmania in 1888. At the time of his enlistment he was living in Avoca, Tasmania.

Captain Clarence Smith Jeffries, 34th Battalion, was an officer of high repute and from whom great things were expected. This twenty-three year old officer had been wounded in June at Messines but was back in action on the 12th October when the 34th Battalion, part of the 9th Brigade, began their advance on two objectives which would take them north of Tyne Cot, beyond the old Roulers railway, and close to Passchendaele itself. His leadership had helped secure the first objective, an enemy garrison holding the pill-box at Hillside Farm where thirty-five prisoners were taken. A couple of hours later while advancing onto the second objective north of Defy Crossing, a machine-gun firing from the right near Decline Copse on the old railway bank began to take its toll on his men. Without hesitation Captain Jeffries with several of his men, headed straight for the gun. As they neared it Captain Jeffries was hit and he died, never knowing he would be awarded the Victoria Cross for his magnificent effort. This gallant action by Captain Jeffries and his men helped eliminate another obstacle to the general advance along the crest of the Passchendaele Ridge.

Clarence Smith Jeffries was born in Wallsend, New South Wales in 1894. At the time of his enlistment he was a mine surveyor from Abermain, New South Wales.

Following the concentration of British military graves in the years following the war, Captain Jeffries and Sergeant McGee were buried near each other in the Tyne Cot British Military cemetery - they had both fallen on the same day, the 12th October 1917.

The Australian and New Zealand Divisions, seeking to use the high, drying ground on the ridges stemming west and south-west of Passchendaele village, had to give way as exhaustion, brought about through constant, ferocious fighting in atrocious conditions, gradually overtook them. This led to the Canadians being fed into the line to replace them in the preparations for the massive November offensive destined to capture the Ridge and the infamous village of Passchendaele. This final action brought the fighting around Ypres to its close for the winter.

When McGee and Jeffries fell at Passchendaele, their deaths heralded the close of the Australian effort near Ypres for 1917. They were the last members of the Australian infantry to gain the highest award for gallantry bestowed on the Australians for the period June to October 1917 - Messines to Passchendaele.

The Victoria Cross awards to Private Inwood, Sergeant McGee and Captain Jeffries were just three of the nine awarded to the Australian Imperial Forces during that June to October period.

The following list of those who gained this highest of awards for gallantry does not include the name of Major F. H. Tubbs of the 7th Battalion who fell at Polygon Wood on the 20th September 1917.

His was awarded for supreme gallantry at Lone Pine on the 9th August 1915 during the Gallipoli campaign. Major Tubbs is buried at Remi Sidings, Lijssenthoek Military Cemetry, Poperinghe.

Victoria Cross Awards to the Australian Imperial Force for the period June to October 1917.

Captain R.C. Grieve, 37th Battalion.
Messines 7th June 1917
(Died in Melbourne, Australia - 4th October. 1957)

Private J. Carroll, 33rd Battalion.
St. Yves, Messines 7th to 12th June 1917
(Died in Perth, Australia - 4th October. 1971)

2nd Lieutenant F. Birks, MM, 6th Battalion.
Glencorse Wood 20th September 1917
(Buried in Perth Military Cemetery, Zillebeke, Belgium)

Private R.R. Inwood, 10th Battalion.
Polygon Wood 19th to 22nd September 1917
(Died in Adelaide, Australia - 23rd October.1971)

Sergeant J.J. Dwyer, 4th Company. Australian M.G.C.
Zonnebeke 26th September 1917
(Died in Tasmania, Australia - 17th January.1962)

Private P. Bugden, 31st Battalion.
Polygon Wood 26th to 28th September 1917
(Buried in Hooge Crater Cemetery, Hooge, Belgium)

Sergeant L. McGee, 40th Battalion.
Tyne Cot 4th October 1917
(Buried in Tyne Cot Cemetery, Passchendaele, Belgium)

Captain C. S. Jeffries, 34th Battalion.
Passchendaele 12th October 1917
(Buried in Tyne Cot Cemetery, Passchendaele, Belgium)

Lance Corporal W. Peeler B.E.M., 3rd Pioneers.
Gravenstafel 20th September to 4th October 1917
(Died in Victoria, Australia - 23rd May 1968)

INWOOD, REGINALD ROY, Private, served in
the European War in France, and was awarded the
Victoria Cross (London Gazette, 26th Nov. 1917 :
*"No.6506, Reginald Roy Inwood, Private 10th Battn.
Australian Imperial Force. For most conspicuous bravery and devotion to duty during the advance to the second objective. He moved forward, through our barrage
alone to an enemy strong post and captured it, together
with nine prisoners, killing several of the enemy. During
the evening he volunteered for a special all-night patrol,
which went out 600 yards in front of our line, and there
- by his coolness and sound judgement - obtained and
sent back very valuable information as to the enemy's
movements. In the early morning of 21 Sept. Private
Inwood located a machine gun which was causing several casualties. He went out alone and bombed the gun
and team, killing all but one, whom he brought in as a
prisoner with the gun."*

The V.C. and D.S.O. The Standard Art Book Co. Ltd., 1924

McGEE, LEWIS, Sergt., served in France, and was posthumously awarded the Victoria Cross (London Gazette, 26 Nov. 1917) : *"Lewis McGee, No. 456, Sergt., late 40th Battn. Australian Imperial Force. For most conspicuous bravery. When, in the advance to the final objective, Sergt. McGee led his platoon with great dash and bravery, though strongly opposed, and under heavy shell fire. His platoon was suffering severely and the advance of the Company was stopped by machine-gun fire from a 'Pill-box' post. Single-handed Sergt. McGee rushed the post armed only with a revolver. He shot some of the crew and captured the rest, and thus enabled the advance to proceed. He reorganised the remnants of his platoon, and was foremost in the remainder of the advance, and during consolidation of the position he did splendid work. This non-commissioned officer's coolness and bravery were conspicuous and contributed largely to the success of the company's operations. Sergt. McGee was subsequently killed in action."*

The V.C. and D.S.O. The Standard Art Book Co. Ltd., 1924

JEFFRIES, CLARENCE SMITH, Capt., served in the European War, and for his gallantry while serving in France was awarded a posthumous Victoria Cross (London Gazette, 18 Dec. 1917) : *"Clarence Smith Jeffries, Capt., late 34th Battn. Australian Imperial Force. For most conspicuous bravery in attack, when his company was held up by enemy machine-gun fire from concrete emplacements. Organising a party, he rushed one emplacement, capturing four machine-guns and thirty-five prisoners. He then led his company forward under extremely heavy enemy artillery barrage and enfilade machine-gun fire to the objective. Later, he again organised a successful attack on a machine-gun emplacement, capturing two machine-guns and thirty more prisoners. This gallant officer was killed during the attack, but it was entirely due to his bravery and initiative that the centre of the attack was not held up for a lengthy period. His example had a most inspiring influence."*

The V.C. and D.S.O. The Standard Art Book Co. Ltd., 1924

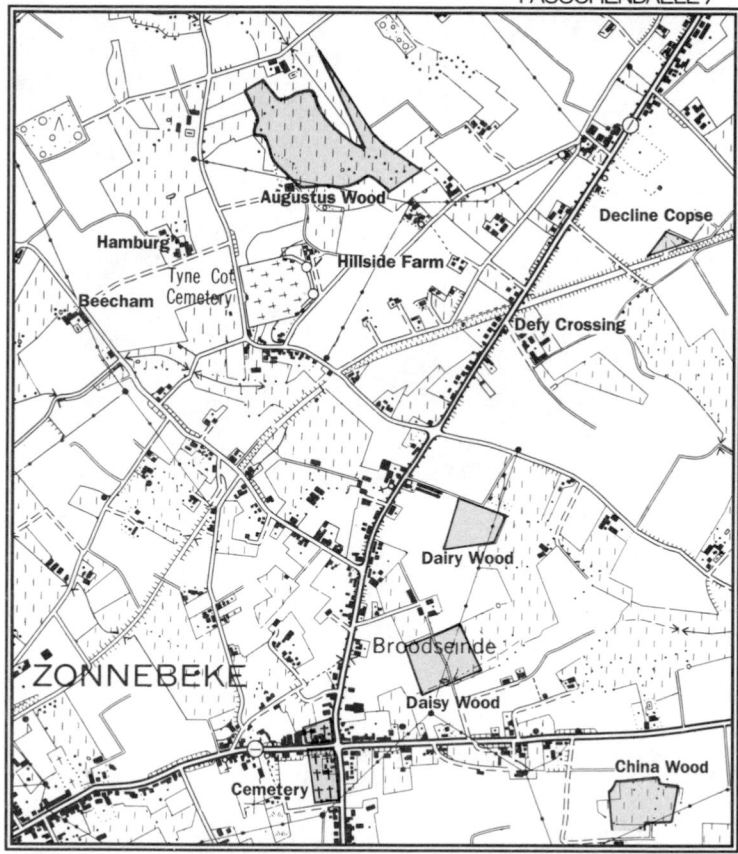

This area on the lower slopes of the Passchendaele ridge shows the locations of the strongpoint positions Beecham, Hamburg and Hillside close to Tyne Cot British Cemetery where Sergeant McGee and Captain Jeffries were destined to win the highest award for gallantry, and where they were both to be killed in action. Augustus wood, Defy Crossing, Decline Copse, Dairy Wood and Daisy Wood, also close to these positions, show just how condensed was the area of operations north of the Broodseinde crossroads during that fateful month of October 1917.

109

Part of the Hillside pill-box defences, where Captain Jeffries courageous action was a major factor in the award of his Victoria Cross, maintains the position it held in 1917. Although a remnant of its former self and an eyesore in the garden of the farm standing on the site of the original Hillside Farm, it retains an air of menace with a clear view of Passchendaele church to its rear, and a commanding view of the ground over which the Australians had to advance. What is left of the pill-box is just one wall, now lying flat on the ground, belying its original size. The retired couple who inhabit this quiet little farmhouse on the high ground to the left of the road at the junction of the old Roulers railway and the road to Passchendaele, known during the Great War as Defy Crossing, have an interesting tale to tell on the post war history of the pill-box. Local people used it as an air-raid shelter during the second world war and, at that time, it housed the water pump seen in the foreground, an indication of how well organised were the German defences. It has since been used as a source of flint and aggregate for building purposes, gradually being reduced to its present size, which would suggest it to have been no more than small pill-box. A closer look, and the knowledge that it formed one wall of a formidable construction, gives some idea of what Capt. Jeffries and his men faced on the 12th October 1917.

OFFICERS WILSDON AND RAE
(Reference page 46)

O F the five officers of the 10th Battalion who took part in the Celtic Wood operation only two were able to make a safe return to the Australian lines, according to the official records. They were Lieutenants R. P. James (Renmark, S. Australia) and T. B. Laurie (Salisbury, S. Australia). Both had been wounded and had lain out between the opposing positions for several hours. A third officer, Second Lieutenant W. H. Wilsdon, D. C. M. (Caltowie, S. Australia) who was operating near the eastern edge of the wood, just disappeared in the maelstrom of close combat. This officer was never heard of again. He was officially posted as missing and commemorated on the Menin Gate Memorial to the Missing at Ypres together with the raid commander, Lieutenant F. J. Scott (Gawler, S. Australia), who was seen to fall and, as with Lieutenant Wilsdon, his body was never recovered. One of the wounded officers, Lieutenant B. L. Laurie, died of wounds in the April of 1918 and is buried at Caestre Military Cemetery, France. There is no way of telling whether his wounds were those received at Celtic Wood, but it is highly unlikely that they were.

Also listed on the panels of the Menin Gate Memorial, a vast edifice to the missing, are twenty other ranks who took part in the raid and whose bodies were never found. The battalion and brigade records of the period seem a little scanty to us today but, after all, it was a time for traumatic activity and action, and not for recording. Consequently the full list of the eighty-five who took part, and specifically of those who fell in the raid, is not available to us today. As for the remaining officer, twenty-one-year-old Second Lieutenant A. N. Rae (Kilkenny, S. Australia), he was certainly known to have been killed in the wood. His grave can be found today in Tyne Cot Military Cemetery.

Following the war when agricultural activity became once more the concern of the area, members of the farming community were forever finding dug-out entrances, traces of war and lonely, isolated graves or soldiers' remains. Evidently the body of Second Lieutenant Rae, together with those of five other ranks, were discovered during this period because they are now buried in Military Cemeteries within the Ypres Salient as are so many men of the British and Dominion armies. When, and by whom, their bodies were found is not known as records do not detail information of this nature. So, as far as we know, these are the only dead of the Celtic Wood raiders from C Company who have identifiable graves. How many of the unknown soldiers buried in multitude of cemeteries in this area of the Salient are their comrades from that raid on the 9th October? Only God in his Wisdom knows.

Those whose bodies were not found probably lie in peace in a mass grave or isolated glory somewhere beneath or around the brooding ridge. "The fortunes of war'" is often quoted as a way of summing-up results of violent conflict. "The unfortunates of war" is a more meaningful description relating to soldiers dying in action - and particularly so with the fallen at Celtic Wood.

Ted Smith

German strongpoints Hamburg and Beecham, major obstacles to the Australian advance in October 1917. Their proximity to Tyne Cot is shown in this photograph taken from the British Military cemetery. Beecham is the farm to the left and Hamburg the one to the right. A view from this point in October 1917 would have witnessed the exploits of Sergeant McGee of the 40th Battalion which culminated in his award of the Victoria Cross. Sergeant McGee was killed in action a few days later on the 12th October at Augustus Wood about 500 metres further up the ridge.

Ted Smith

Defy Crossing was an exposed position where the old Roulers-Ypres railway crossed the Passchendaele - Broodseinde road. The Australian advance on Passchendaele petered-out around this spot in mid-October 1917. The copse in the distance along the old embankment was called Decline Copse during the war, and it was while moving to attack a machine-gun post firing from this copse that Captain C. Jeffries was killed on the 12th October 1917. He was awarded a posthumous V.C. for this action.

Ted Smith

Remnants of the famous bunker at Hillside Farm where the garrison of 25 men plus 2 machine-guns were captured by Captain C. Jeffries, 34th Battalion, on the 12th October 1917. Captain Jeffries was awarded a posthumous V.C. later in the day after being killed in action while attacking a machine-gun post in Decline Copse. The group of trees in the centre distance mark the site of Augustus Wood, close to Passchendaele, where Sergeant McGee V.C., 40th Battalion, was killed in action on October the 12th 1917.

Taken from Defy Crossing, this photograph shows the low ridge that was the 2nd Objective on the 12th October 1917. Captain Jeffries, 34th Battalion, was moving across this field to the objective when machine-gun fire from Decline Copse, the group of trees in the distant right, started to take its toll of the advancing Australians. He and some of his men immediately turned toward the copse and attacked the machine-gun post. It was during this action that Captain Jeffries was killed and was awarded a posthumous Victoria Cross. The monument seen left of the middle distance on the crest of the ridge commemorates the action of the Canadian 85th Battalion (Nova Scotia).

Ted Smith

Zonnebeke church from the Broodseinde Crossroads, 1990. This section of the crossroads was the site of a large German military cemetery during the war.

Australian wounded at a Collecting Post on the Menin Road near Birr Cross Roads, September 1917, before being cleared for transport back to hospitals in the rear towards Poperinghe.

APPENDIX I.

REPORT OF THE RAID BY THE 11TH AND 12TH BATTALIONS (3RD BRIGADE)

Document No. 128. 7/10/17
(Reference page 38)

REPORT OF RAID BY 11TH AND 12TH BATTALIONS
(3RD BRIGADE)

<u>SECRET.</u>

<u>Report by Major A. Steele. c/o 11th Batt.</u>

1. Order to raid Celtic Copse in conjunction with 12th Batt., was received at 15.43 on 6th October 1917. I at once consulted with Major Darrel "A" Coy. and arranged for a party consisting of Lt.'s Vowels and Gudgeon and 30 other ranks to be held in readiness.

2. Immediately after making the arrangements I went to 12th Batt., and saw the Commander, Lt. Col. Elliot DSO, who kindly allowed me to issue the orders and be responsible for the raid.

3. Composition of the raiding party was as attached order No. 32

4. Brigades message No. AWH 355 required zero hour to be delayed until midnight, was not received by 11th Batt. until 23.07.

5. Arrangements for covering fire of Artillery, Stokes Mortars and Vickers/Lewis guns are shown on attached order No. 32.

6. At 00.02 what seemed to be only one battery of 18 pounders commenced a desultory fire on the arranged lines. Their effect was so feeble that the 2nd Machine Gun Coy. guns who were to assist in the box barrage, did not think that it was time to commence, and we thus lost very valuable support.

7. Although rather in doubt as to whether, or not, the barrage was down, Lt. Vowels, 11th Batt. O/C Raid, led the party forward at 00.02 am. This officer moved into the woods with such vigor that the enemy was completely suprised, and most were caught in their funk holes and killed or captured quite easily.

8. At 00.10 the return signal was fired, and by 00.25 O/C Raid had reported by wire that he had been successful. A preliminary report was sent to Brigade at 00.40 on 7/10/17.

9. By 00.40 O/C Raid had reported to Brigade and all the 11th Batt. portion of the raid had come in. Contrary to my own orders the 12th Batt. portion of the raid did not report back to Brigade via my Battalion, nor have I had any report from 12th Batt. O/C Raid, Lt. Davey. I later learned that C/O 12th Batt. reported that their portion of the raid had in fact taken 10 prisoners and 1 machine gun. Their casualties were - 1 other rank wounded.

10 Results

Prisoners of 448th Regt.	12 other ranks.	
Secured during raid by 11th Batt. patrol.	3 other ranks.	
Total	15 other ranks.	
Machine Guns	1.	
Estimated enemy killed	20. (11th Batt. portion only)	
Enemy wounded	30.	
Identification of units opposite	Complete.	

Our Casualties.

Killed	None.
Wounded	2. (11th Batt. - 1) (12th Batt. - 2)

11. Summary

a) I am of the opinion that ample time was given to the artillery to arrange their barrage for zero at 23.00. The one hour postponement owing to difficulty of communication forward might have spelt failure, and did mean the raid party had to lie out in No-Man's Land for one hour!

b) When put down, the fire of the guns was so feeble as to be
    negligible.

c) The 3rd A.L.T.M. battery of 2 guns (Trench Mortars) under Lt.
    Miles rendered valuable assistance.

d) The guns of the 2nd Aust. M.G. Coy. did not come into action
    owing to not knowing when the barrage was down.

e) If the box barrage as per my order had been even reasonably
    carried out by the artillery, many of the enemy who were seen
    running away from the eastern side of the wood, must have be-
    come casualties, or at least forced to surrender.

f) Prisoners cross examined stated that 2 Lieut's., 150 other ranks,
    and machine guns were in Celtic Wood. They also state that
    the vigour of our attack surprised them, and left them with lit-
    tle chance to resist.

g) The ground crossed was marshy and very heavy going.

I would like to sum up by stating that the success of the raid seems
due to the skill and energy of the officers (particularly Lt. Vowels),
to the good arrangements and accurate fire of the 3rd A.L.T.M.
battery, and the fine spirits of the men concerned.
    I desire finally, to bring to the notice of Brigade, the excellent
work done in the above raid by :

Lt. P.E.M. Vowels. - 11th Batt.
Lt. A.H. Miles. - 3rd A.L.T.M. Battery.

(Sgd.) A. Steele.

Major
C/O. 11th Batt. (Australian)

12TH BATT. VERSION OF CELTIC RAID 6/7th OCTOBER 1910 BY 2/Lt. DAVEY A.S.L. C/O RAID 12th BATT.

a) My party consisted of Sgt. Cherry and 10 men of "B" Coy. plus Corp. Miller and 15 men of "C" Coy.

b) We formed up and started to move out of our front line trench at 22.45 when word was received that the barrage would not start until 24.00.

c) We stayed out front in shell holes until our 18 pounders opened up and then we advanced. We only went 100 yards into the wood, and then came back when 2 rockets were fired from our front line.

d) We did not observe much wire or front trench. Three dug-outs were bombed. These were fairly deep underground and had staircases. We captured a machine gun plus 10 men who we took prisoner. One man who was about to fire at us was shot. The wood appeared to be only lightly held, and there was very little resistance. We did not see many concrete pill-boxes. One man reported seeing a field gun fire at us through a concrete emplacement concealed in an old farm building just on the edge of the wood. It fired through the rafters and was protected by machine guns.

e) The ground was very wet and swampy, and the wood itself badly knocked about. I did hear, but did not see the 11th Batt. party after the advance began.

f) Casualties.   1 other rank wounded.

(Sgd.) A.S.L. Davey. 2/Lt.
         "C" Coy. 12th Batt. (Australian)

Although this raid by the 11th and 12th Battalions had a surprise factor, their view of the suppporting barrage had elements of the same controversy which was to attend the tragic efforts of their comrades from the 10th Battalion forty-eight hours later at the same spot. Both operations do not seem to have been accorded the supporting fire that was warranted if success was to be achieved. Notwithstanding that, the raid on the 7th October would be a signal success, and would only last twenty minutes or so. The wood was penetrated, prisoners taken, dug-outs bombed and a machine-gun captured, with only two men wounded, and all within the twenty minutes mentioned above! They were back within their own lines and the raid report had been sent off to Brigade within another twenty minutes. A totally successful raid having taken, from move-out time to the file report time, a total of forty minutes. Sadly, Major Steele, Commanding officer of the 11th Battalion, who wrote and filed the main report, was killed by shellfire on the evening of the raid day and was buried just behind the Australian front line. His body was never recovered and his name appears on the Menin Gate Memorial at Ypres. The raid hero, Lieutenant P. Vowels, was killed in action in the Hazebrouck area in May 1918. He lies in the Borre British Military Cemetery near Hazebrouck.

On the 9th October the luckless 10th Battalion, with a far larger party under the valiant Lieutenant Scott, would attempt to create a diversion of sorts in the same wood for their comrades of the 2nd Australian Division and II Anzac Corps who were attacking farther north. The venue and immediate objectives were similar to those of the 11th and 12th Battalions but the result was tragic and their supreme sacrifice did little to aid their northern attacking colleagues.

Officers prominent in the
11th Battalion A.I.F. raid on CELTIC WOOD
7th October, 1917

Register reference - The Menin Gate Memorial, Ypres

Steele, Maj. Alexander, *DSO., DCM.*
11th Bn. 7th Oct., 1917. Age 29. Son of Dugald and
Elizabeth Burton Steele, of "Muirhome", Mount Gambier,
South Australia.

Major Steele was killed by shell fire on the evening of the
raid, 7th October. He was in the vicinity of the crater and
large pill-box on the crest of the ridge when the shelling
occurred. He was killed immediately and buried beside the
crater. After the war his grave was never found and he is
commemorated on the 11th Battalion panel on the Menin
Gate Memorial to the Missing at Ypres. He was the officer
who planned the raid, a joint operation with the 12th Battalion, and he monitored its execution.

Register reference - Borre British Cemetery, France.

Vowels, Lt. Phillip Edward Michael, MC *and Bar.*
11th Bn. Australian Inf. Killed in Action 11th May, 1918.
Age 27. Son of William Henry and Bridget M. Vowels, of
407, William Street, Perth, Western Australia. Native of
Horsham, Victoria, Australia.
Plot I. Row A. Grave 33.

Lieutenant Vowels led the 11th Battalion raiders with great
vigour and expertise. On Major Steele's report he was
awarded the Military Cross and won a Bar to this during the
furious fighting of the following year. Lieutenant Vowels
was killed in action on the 11th May 1918 in the immediate area of Hazebrouck and the Forest of Nieppe.

The foregoing register entries have been reproduced with the kind permission of
the Commonwealth War Graves Commission, Maidenhead, Berkshire.

119

"The man of Pick and Shovel. Pioneer 1917". From a lithograph by Daryl Lindsay.

APPENDIX II

TENTH INFANTRY BATTALION A.I.F.
ORDER FOR RAID ON
CELTIC WOOD

Document 130.
(Reference page 39)

SECRET.   Copy No.......

TENTH INFANTRY BATTALION A.I.F.
ORDER FOR RAID ON CELTIC WOOD

1. INTENTION. "C" Company, 10th Battalion plus reinforcements will raid that part of CELTIC WOOD between D.30.C.00.65 to D.29.D.8.6. to D.29.D.7.5. to D.29.D.75.35 to D.30.C.00.45.

2. DATE. X Day

3. TIME. Zero hour to be notified later. Party to return to their trench by Zero plus 30 minutes.

4. RAID COMMANDER. Lieut. F. J. Scott.

5. METHOD. Four parties of 2 Officers and 25 Other Ranks, plus 6 Trench Mortar Battery personnel.

6. OBJECT. To destroy dugouts in that part of the wood to be raided, kill enemy, and procure sufficient prisoners for identification purposes. Capture enemy machine guns and documents.

7. ARTILLERY ETC. Three batteries will be concentrated on wood from zero to zero plus 10. 3rd. A.L.T.M.B. will concentrate on road from D.29.D.8.6. to D.29.92.40. from zero plus 4 to zero plus 8. Raiding troops will advance close up to barrage. 3rd. Machine Gun Company will provide flanking fire to protect both flanks of area to be raided.

8. DRESS. Rifle and bayonet, Bandolier, 50 rounds S.A.A., Loaded magazines, and 4 bombs per man. 5 men per party will be equipped as rifle grenadiers and carry 8 rifle grenades per man.

9. ADMINISTRATION ARRANGEMENTS. In order to provide a jumping off line for the raid party, "C" Company plus reinforcements will relieve "D" Company less Lewis Guns and teams, during night preceeding X day, "D" Company moving back to

occupy trench vacated by "C" Company. As soon as raiding party has moved out to attack, "D" Company will re-occupy front line trench occupied by "C" Coy. before jumping off. On completion of raid "C" Company will move back to their original trench in support. "A" and "B" Companies will be prepared to support party giving covering machine-gun fire on country on right of CELTIC WOOD if necessary. "D" Company will be prepared to give covering fire on ground on left if necessary.

10. Reports to Battalion Headquarters.

11. ACKNOWLEDGE.

Lieut. Colonel

Commdg. Tenth Infantry Battalion A.I.F.

Issued by runner on 8/10/17 at 1800, to :-

Copy No.

1 LOOK.
2 LOIN.
3 "A" Coy.
4 "B" Coy.
5 "C" Coy.
6 "D" Coy.
7 Border Regt.
8 File.
9 C.O.
10 C.O.
11 War Diary.
12 "   "
13 "   "
14 Spare.

"Another journey to the Gun Pits". From a Lithograph by Daryl Lindsay.

APPENDIX III.

PASSCHENDAELE
THE GERMAN PERSPECTIVE
(Reference page 46)

THE criticism often levelled against modern military writers describing the 1917 battles around Ypres is that they
reflect with emphasis on the trials and tribulations suffered
by the armies of Britain and her dominions, and that Field
Marshal Haig and his commanders somehow allowed the
enemy forces to withdraw almost unscathed. Whatever we,
in retrospect, feel about the Field Marshal's conduct and
handling of the battles, it is certainly not the case that the
enemy was allowed to withdraw unscathed.

In disregarding what was happening to the German soldier
in the field, influential writers including those such as Lloyd
George and Liddell Hart, have allowed a slightly flawed impression of the battles to be presented.

It is very true that the British forces did suffer severely
throughout the bruising campaign to unlock the German
grip on the Ypres salient. Fighting over swampy, broken
ground and in notoriously obscene conditions, they did sus-
tain heavy losses in men and materials - how could they fail
to. However, we must not forget that the German armies in
Flanders suffered even more severely. On examining the

pain and suffering inflicted on them one can perceive the battle to have been *"a near run thing"* for them. How fortunate to their cause was the break in the weather which turned the already unspeakable conditions of the battleground into an almost impassable quagmire. The cherished hope by the British of a major breakthrough may well have borne fruition had not nature intervened.

General von Kuhl, Chief of Staff to the northern group of German armies opposing the British in Flanders, wrote :

"The hell of Verdun was surpassed. In the water-filled craters cowered the defenders, without shelter from the weather, hunger, and cold, abandoned without hope to the overwhelming fire."

He was only stating the obvious as he saw it back at high command. He went even further, writing :

"Unlike the Somme in 1916, the Flanders' battles consumed the German strength to such a degree that the damage inflicted on us could no longer be repaired."

The luckless British also suffered and existed in those same water-filled craters but, because their artillery, honed to a supreme battlefield weapon, was far superior to that of the enemy at that time, they were not subjected to such devastating fire as that which rained down on the Germans.

The German official history of the period, *Flanderen 1917*, states that no less than eighty-six German divisions had been involved in the fighting, and twenty-two of these had been committed twice, so heavy was the strain on the German strength. This mauling was the price being extracted from one of the greatest armies the world had ever seen.

"Divisions disappeared by dozens into the turmoil of battle, only to emerge from the witches' cauldron after a short period thinned, exhausted and often reduced to a miserable remnant .

... significant signs of strain manifested themselves."

General Ludendorff voiced a great concern as Chief of

Staff to the German Military Forces when he stated :

"Our wastage has been so high as to cause misgivings, and exceeded all expectations. Certain units no longer triumphed over the demoralising effect of the defensive battles as they have done formerly."

On the 11th October 1917, Crown Prince Rupprecht recorded in his diary :

"Most perturbing is the fact that our troops are steadily deteriorating."

When, after the Armistice, Sir John Elliot, a post war observer of the scene, went to Germany to examine the divisional and unit records of those taking part, he concluded that it appeared that, during the winter campaign in Flanders in 1917 :

"The German army was very near to disintegration."

Interested observers should not confuse the German army of 1917 with that of 1918. With the knowledge of having just held together through the cruellest of fighting, and bolstered with the strength of the fifty to sixty divisions released from the Russian front, the German army of 1918 was something different altogether from that of 1917.

It was this new, fresh, confident army taking advantage of spring weather and firm, dry ground which would spearhead the drive to Amiens, pushing the thin screen of Gough's Fifth Army before them - and they harboured no nightmares of the disasters of the Flanders fighting.

To sum up, a German General Staff publication has stated that, during the winter of 1917-18 :

"Germany had been brought near to certain destruction by the Flanders battles of 1917."

The fickle Belgian weather, together with the Russians, had seen to it that this did not occur.

This constituent of reality must be included in any balanced study of the battles for Passchendaele as must the damage inflicted on the German armies during this period have its bearing on any study on the final victory in 1918.

As far as the damage caused in 1917 is concerned, there can be no doubt as to the contribution to it played by the five Australian divisions employed by General Plumer's Second Army. Taking into account the size of their force, and the fact that they were only used once from mid-September to mid-October, then no amount of praise can be enough to honour the Australian efforts.

Their methods may have been unorthodox, their style not always in line with strict military codes, meaning they did not always stand on ceremony, as befitted the general Anzac way of life. Nevertheless there could be no denying their extreme efficiency and value as great soldiers and elite troops! The enemy always held them in very high regard, as must be said he did the troops from the other dominions of Canada, New Zealand and South Africa. One very general post-battle analysis placed the Guards Division and the Scottish battalions who had taken part in the battle amongst the very best they had met in the field. However a more considered opinion might have indicated that no one had contributed more to the development of the battle, and the consequent trials of the German Army, than the Australian units taking part. Used sparingly but potently, the Ansacs had torn great gaps, and scored some stunning victories in the German's central position, overcoming many obstacles to become masters in their field of operations.

Even though great honour and many more victories would come their way during the dramatic and dark days of 1918, it might be argued that the period September to October 1917 saw the men from Down Under invincible along the Broodseinde Ridge, at their magnificent best

APPENDIX IV.

ARTILLERY DEBATE
CORRESPONDENCE.
(Reference page 50)

THE documents detailed in this appendix follow the post-battle correspondence between the 1st Australian Division and their artillery support from the 5th Australian Division. The documents are from the private collection of Dr. John Laffin and the Public Records Office, Kew, London.

(1)

"B" GROUP ARTILLERY

SECRET   Headquarters,
                                        8th October 1917
D.A.H.Q.
 5th Aus.Divn.

The G. O. C. 3rd Infantry Brigade has requested that Artillery attention be given to JOINERS AVENUE in J 6 c and the Cemetry in J 6 a during the operations on "X" day.

He considers that these are points which may be troublesome during the operations which he proposes to conduct against CELTIC WOOD.

As this is on the 7th Division front and this group has its task already allotted, could this matter be arranged, please?

(Sgd.) A. Caddy.

Lieut - Colonel,
Commanding "B" Group prty.

The Brigade Major, 5th. D. A. informed me
verbally that this would be done.

Adjutant 13th F.A. 5th Aus.Div.

(2)

3rd. AUSTRALIAN INFANTRY BRIGADE.

SECRET   G1101
                                                             11.10.17

1st Aus. Div.

Regarding the raid by 10th Battalion on CELTIC WOOD on the 9th. inst., I have to report that the Artillery co-operation was not as satisfactory as it might have been.

My orders were to deal with the Artillery Liaison Officer in arranging for the support I required.

This Officer - (Major McCormack of 5th. Divisional Artillery) told me that one of the two Groups covering my front had been alloted to cover the front of the 2nd. Division. I asked him if the group left with me was complete in guns, and he replied that they were. His C.O. agreed to the following arrangements, viz :- to place 3 batteries on to CELTIC WOOD, i. e. between D 29 d 8 3 and D 29 d 70 65. while the remaining three batteries barraged a line across the Brigade front. The rate of fire was to be 4 rounds per gun per minute till plus 16 when it was to be reduced. At plus 16 the batteries covering the WOOD were to spread across the whole front.

The barrage line and timetable were to be as per barrage map issued in connection with the major operation on the same day.

It was also arranged for the 4.5" howitzers to operate on the rear end of the WOOD and then to spread at plus 16.

The 7th Division were to operate on JOINERS AVENUE and the gully just North of it.

All these arrangements were promised verbally and Artillery orders were to follow.

At about 9.30pm on the 8th inst. the Artillery orders were shewn to me by the Liaison Officer. These orders shewed only five batteries firing and the tasks allotted did not agree with the verbal arrangements. Only two batteries were firing on the frontage between D 27 d 7 0 and about D 29 d 5 8 (these co-ordinates are only approximate as I have had no copy of the orders).

This decreased the density of fire on this WOOD from about 11 yards to about 33 yards per gun.

Furthermore the rate of fire was reduced to three rounds per gun after Zero plus 4 and still further reduced later.

I complained to the Liaison Officer who rang up his C.O. I was then assured that the barrage would be thickened up as desired and that the rate of fire would be increased.

I was also assured that all the batteries covering my front were up to strength in guns.
At Zero the Artillery opened fire but the barrage did not come up to expectations. Those who saw it affirm that the number of shells fired was not as arranged.

(2).

The No. of guns in operation make it appear that the barrage was not as promised to me.

Might I ask that the following questions be answered by the Group Commander, please.

(1)   How many guns operated on this occasion ?
(2)   What rate of fire was maintained ?
(3)   What was the distribution of tasks of the various batteries ?
(4)   Did the 4.5" Howitzers fire as requested to do ?
(5)   Were the original orders amended according to my request on the night 8/9th. and did these orders reach the batteries in time for them to alter their arrangements ?

The raid incurred heavy casualties in my party and I consider that these casualties would not have been so heavy if the Artillery arrangements had been as arranged.

(Sgd.) Bennet..

Brig-General.
Commanding 3rd Aus. Infantry Brigade.

(3)

CONFIDENTIAL.

FIRST AUSTRALIAN DIVISION.

	Divisional Headquarters,
124/99.	12th October 1917.

5th Aust. Div.

The attached letter from the G.O.C., 3rd Aus. Inf. Bde. is for-warded to you, as the 5th Aus. Div. Arty. has now returned to your Command.

I should be very much obliged if you could cause inquiries to be made into the circumstances detailed therein which occured while the 5th Div. Arty. was working under this H.Q.

(Sgd.) H. B. Walker,

Major-Gen.
Commanding 1st Australian Division.

5th Aus. Div.
  G14/2250.

C. R. A.
              I am directed to ask for a report on this matter, please.

(Sgd.) J. H. Peck Lt-Col

13.10.17   General Staff 5th Aus. Div.

(4)

CONFIDENTIAL

SG/24

FIFTH AUSTRALIAN DIVISIONAL ARTILLERY.

Headquarters,
13th October 1917.

C.O. "B" Group.

Forwarded to you.
The C.R.A. directs me to ask you for an early report on this matter, please, and also one from Major P. J. McCormack.

(Sgd.) H. Hulton Major.

Brigade Major.
5th Australian Divisional Artillery.

(5)

"B" GROUP ARTILLERY.

CONFIDENTIAL.

D.A.H.Q.
5th Aus. Div.

Headquarters,
14th October 1917.

Referring to the attached statement from G.O.C., 3rd Aus. Infantry Brigade that the Artillery support given by this group to the raid by his 10th Battalion on 9.10.17 was not as arranged, I respectfully wish to say that this assumption is wrong.

The facts are that all requests made by him were actually carried out.

Copies of the order issued for this operation, of Signal messages, and a map shewing zones are attached from which it will be seen that all eight batteries of the Group were allotted tasks and not only five as stated by the Brigadier, 3rd Inf. Bde.

In addition to the tasks shewn in the order, three Howitzers were concentrated on CELTIC WOOD. These instructions were given personally by me to the Battery Commander.

It will thus be seen that the zone covering CELTIC WOOD had two 18pdr. batteries, each of 6 guns, portions of two other batteries (the 53rd. with 3 and the 49th with 5 guns) superimposed, searching through CELTIC WOOD; also both Howitzer batteries with five (5) guns each and the 50th Bty (of only 2 guns) forming a barrage 200 yards in rear of the 18 pdr. batteries and lifting with them, three of the Hows. actually firing into CELTIC WOOD.

Therefore 15-18pdr. covered a front of 250 yards (from D 29 d 7 0 to D 29 d 75 60) making a density of fire on CELTIC WOOD of 1 - 18 pdr. gun per 17 yards. The three Howitzers in rear of the WOOD reduce this figure to one gun or How. per 14 yards on this frontage.

This was a big percentage of the number of guns in action and it left the flanks very thinly covered but as the Brigadier had had this pointed out to him by both Liaison Officers at my instruction and stated that he could deal with this himself, it was arranged as he desired.

The request for action on JOINERS AVENUE and the Cemetery was referred to 5th Aus. D.A.H.Q. (copy of letter attached) as these places were in the 7th. Division zone.

2. The order referred to by the Brigadier, 3rd Inf. Bde. was amended as he desired. This order was issued before the alterations could be made, therefore the alterations were wired and acknowledgements received.

3. I am pleased to have the opportunity of answering the questions asked as it makes the matter clearer. The following are the replies :-

   1. 26 - 18 pdr.guns)   10 - 18 pdrs. and 2 - Hows. being
       10 - 4.5" Hows)   out of action for various reasons.

   2. Four (4) rounds per gun or How. until Zero plus 16 mins. as requested by the Brigadier.

   3. As stated above and shewn in the order, messages and map attached.

I can understand that the whole barrage may not have come up to expectations of the Infantry when it is considered how thinly the flanks were covered, but the CELTIC WOOD portion could not possibly be included in such a statement.

Regarding the paras on the first page of the letter from the G.O.C., 3rd Inf. Bde marked in blue, may fuller particulars be obtained please? As these statements cast grave reflection I desire that this be enquired into.

(Sgd.) A. Caddy

Lieut - Colonel,
Commanding "B" Group Artillery.

(6)

14th October 1917.

The Adjutant,
    "B" Group Artillery,

Regarding the statement of the G.O.C. 3rd Inf. Brigade which has been shewn to me concerning the raid on CELTIC WOOD on the 9th October 1917.

I relieved Major P. J. McCormack at the 3rd Inf. Bde H.Qrs at about 4.15pm on the 8th October, reporting to the G.O.C. 3rd Inf. Brigade. On receipt of "B" Group Operation Memo No.11, I discussed it with the G.O.C. who pointed out that he desired more fire on CELTIC WOOD and referred, in the course of the conversation, to the number of guns in the Group saying that he understood all batteries were complete. I told him that one battery had only two guns in action but that I believed the other batteries would be complete because, coming from the wagon lines to the Inf. Bde. H.Qrs. I knew that efforts were being made to get guns up that night. I did not say that the Group was complete as I was aware of the fact that it was not complete at that time.

The G.O.C. pointed out that he had asked for another battery on CELTIC WOOD and for the rate of fire to be increased to 4 rounds per gun per minute to Zero plus 16, and that this did not agree with the orders.

I spoke to the C.O. "B" Group by telephone who said that both requests would be complied with and pointed out that the flanks of the Divisional Zone were very thinly covered. I explained all this to the Brigadier and discussed it with him, informing him that his requests had been arranged. The position of the Hows. was not discussed.

I left the G.O.C. with the understanding that all had been arranged as he had desired.

(Sgd.) C. M. Chase.
Captain.

No doubt it was the need to husband meagre resources for the main attack on the 12th October that excercised the minds of those given the task of planning what measure of artillery support would be required to assist the raids on the Celtic position carried out by the 11th and 12th Battalions on the 7th October, and the 10th Battalion on the 9th. Perhaps they did err on the side of caution and did not implement or allocate sufficient gunnery to back-up the aforesaid raids. Hence the accusations of thin or weak barrages and all the acrimony that ensued.

The difficulties faced by the gunners would rise to the surface again later in the month when the Canadian Corps would relieve the exhausted Australians and mount the final attempt to secure the ridge, and Passchendaele village itself before winter set-in. The Canadians were singularly successful in their attempts as history has shown and much was owed to the single-minded purpose of their commander, General Currie. Here was a man who would not be hurried even though time was of the essence. He could not and would not be rushed until he was assured that sufficient preparations were in hand to ensure the success and safety of the men under his command. Suitable roads and tracks leading to the front would need to be prepared for the anticipated heavy loads. Sufficient troops, reserves, supplies and guns of all types would have to be made available before he would report to his own commander, Field Marshal Haig, that he and his troops would be ready to move by the 26th October. With such a level of preparation and planning for the forthcoming battle, only the unforeseen and the resilience of the enemy could bar the way to victory. When the attack was launched success was the order of the day culminating in the fall of the village of Passchendaele on the 10th November and the close down of the fighting for the year.

During this period of planning and preparation when the exhausted Australians left the battlefield for a well earned respite after six weeks of continuous action, the incoming Canadians were hard put at times to make any effective sense of what they were taking over, particularly in terms of the all important guns demanded by General Currie.

The following extracts, kindly supplied by John Terraine from his own research archives, illustrates the concern and the mood of the time and may well explain why a certain friction was apparent between the Australian infantry and artillery during the two raids on Celtic Wood.

"The problem of artillery was serious. Currie's G. O. C. Royal Artillery, Brig.-Gen. E. W. B. Morrison, 'had a rude awakening' when a personal reconnaissance prior to taking over the Corps front revealed extensive gun shortages. Of 250 'heavies' to be taken over in situ from the Australians he could find only 227, and of these 89 were out of action. Even worse was the condition of the field artillery. Of 306 18-pounders on paper, less than half were in action, and many of these were 'dotted about in the mud wherever they happened to get bogged'."
Canadian Expeditionary Force 1914-1919. (Official History of the Canadian Army in the First World War) by Col. G. W. L. Nicholson.

"When the Canadian Corps came to count the guns supposed to be taken over on its front more than 100 could not be found. General Currie, on protesting, was assured by higher authorities that, if the guns were missing, which they were loth to believe, he must have been handed indents for them. He replied that he could not fight the Boche with indents, and the requisite number of guns was forthcoming before October 26th."
The Empire at War by Prof. F. H. Underhill, edited by Sir Charles Lucas.

GLOSSARY

A.I.F. - Australian Imperial Force. The name given by Major General Bridges to the main one of two forces raised in 1914. It was an all-volunteer force whose infantry units were connected with the different Australian States. This was not the case with special arms, the artillery, the medical corps and engineers, but the infantry and light horse regiments were recruited from their own States throughout the war. Major General Sir W. T. Bridges K.C.B., C.M.G. commanded the 1st Australian Division, Australian Imperial Force in 1914/15. He died of wounds received in Monash Valley in the Gallipoli Peninsular on 18th May 1915.

ABRAHAM HEIGHTS - A gently rising slope slightly to the north of the road connecting the villages of Zonnebeke and Langemarck. The name came into prominence following the 1915 battles around Ypres. The Germans introduced poison gas to the war for the first time in this sector and that of the Yser canal near Boesinghe and Pilckem. When the Canadians took over a sector their cartographers allocated names with a Canadian connection - *Winnipeg*, *Vancouver*, *Kansas* etc. This piece of high ground was given the name *Abraham Heights* recalling the famous cliffs at Quebec where, two hundred years before, General Wolfe had defeated the French in the bid to secure Canada for the British crown. These heights were taken by the British, New Zealand and Australian infantry after hard fighting during the period September to October 1917.

ANZAC - An abreviation of *Australian and New Zealand Army Corps*. The feats of the Australian and New Zealand troops at Gallipolli made *Anzac* a term of honour and it was made official that it was to be used only for men who had fought at Gallipoli, owing to the loose way people in general used the word for Australians and New Zealanders who had never been there at all. This abreviation eventually became, and still is, the synonym, singular and plural, for addressing Australian and New Zealand troops, regiments, brigades etc.

141

ANZAC RIDGE - A ridge of high ground south-west of Zonnebeke and north of Polygon Wood captured by the Anzac Corps during the Battles of the Menin Road (Third Ypres) in September 1917.

ARMY - *Army* had a specific meaning on the Western Front in the Great War. The original British Expeditionary Force (see B.E.F.) of seven divisions was formed into three Army Corps. On Christmas Day 1914, the term *Army* was introduced and the Army Corps were grouped into two *Armies*. The *First Army* was commanded by Sir Douglas Haig and the *Second Army* by Sir Horace Smith-Dorien. To prevent confusion the word *Army* was dropped from Army Corps which was then termed simply Corps. In September of 1916 the British forces on the Western Front were organised into five *Armies*. Normally exceeding 100,000 men, an *Army* would be commanded by a General. It is customary to write the numerical designation of each *Army* in letters e.g. *First Army*, to use Roman numerals for Corps, e.g. *XI Corps* and Arabic numerals numerals for Divisions, e.g. *5th Division*.

AUGUSTUS WOOD - A small wood on the Passchendaele Ridge north of Tyne Cot Military Cemetery. Heavily fortified by the Germans, Sgt. L. McGee. V.C. 40th Batt. A.I.F. was killed near here in October 1917. Traces of the wood are still to be seen today.

BARRAGE - Artillery fire. To concentrate fire on a line parallel to the front of an infantry attack to destroy the enemy defenses. A concentration of heavy fire in front of advancing or retreating troops to afford them protection.

BOX BARRAGE - A box-barrage was a barrage put-down on three sides, in front and on either flank, of attacking troops to prevent interference by the enemy, leaving the rear open for reinforcements and supports. Likewise, a box-barrage could be laid down on both flanks and to the rear of attacking enemy troops, screening the rear from supports and reinforcements and drawing them on to the defenders weaponry.

BATTALION - Full strength infantry regiment of around 1,000 men including support units. Commanded by a Lieutenant Colonel.

BATTERY - A combat unit of field artillery, generally consisting of 4 or 6 guns, usually commanded by a major. Full strength - 4 gun battery, 198 men. Fighting strength - 138 men.

BEECHAM - A German fortified position, dominated by pill-boxes, built in and around the ruins of a farm on the gentle slopes rising to the Tyne Cot defence system in front of Passchendaele.

B.E.F. - British Expeditionary Force. Expeditionary Force was the official term adopted before the war for the British contingent normally kept available for services overseas in the event of an European war. The first seven divisions sent to France at the beginning of the Great War formed the British Expeditionary Force, later known as the *Contemptibles* and later, by the New Army, as the *Old Contemptibles*. The B.E.F. adopted the name *Contemptible* as a title of honour following an address to the German Army by the Kaiser at Aix la Chappelle on August 19th 1914 - *"It is my Royal and Imperial command that you concentrate your energies, for the immediate present, upon a single purpose, and that is that you address all your skill, and all the valour of my soldiers, to exterminate first the treacherous English and then walk over General French's contemptible little army"*.

BELLEWAARDE - Part of the general commune area of Zillebeke. The area relevant to the fighting around Ypres during the Great War lay just to the north of Hooge Château and the woodland within its grounds called Château Wood. A farm and its outlying land atop the Hooge Ridge, known as *Bellewaarde Farm*, nestling alongside Railway Wood (and the present day memorial to the Royal Engineers missing), was virtually the front line in this area from May 1915 until July 1917. Enemy machine-guns sited amongst the trenches here controlled the whole area along this point and could almost look down the Menin Road right into the gates of Ypres itself. *Bellewaarde Lake*, part of the Hooge Château estate, was continually shelled by both sides until this sector fell to units of the British 8th Division on July 31st 1917 - the opening day of Third Ypres. This ridge is sacred ground to men of the Canadian Princess Patricia's Light Infantry who held it against overwhelming odds in May 1915 during the Second Battle of Ypres. They practically ceased to exist as a regiment for a period following this battle due to the extremely heavy losses incurred. The *Bellewaarde Ridge* is located to the eastern edge of the lake and Château Wood and the fold of ground at the base of its lower slopes marks the beginning of the Westhoek Ridge.

BILLET - A term for soldiers' quarters in a private house or other buildings, usually requisitioned from the local population.

BIRR CROSS ROADS - A military crossing point and Dressing Station at the junction of the military road named *Cambridge Road* and the Menin Road close to Sanctuary Wood. Named by the Leinster Regiment in 1915 after their depôt at Birr in Ireland, a military cemetery of the same name now stands on the spot where those who died at this Dressing Station were originally buried. Other graves were added after the clearing-up operations at the end of the war. The specially constructed log road, known as Military Road. to carry men and supplies through Château Wood to Westhoek started here. Traces of the road remain today as seen in the photograph of the crossroads between pages 112 and 113.

BLIGHTY - England. Home. An everyday word of the old Army in India. The British soldier's version of the Hindustani word *Belati*, itself derived from the Persian word *Wilayut* meaning a province, a country at a distance. It was used on the Western Front with every kind of application. A *Blighty one* was a wound that was sufficiently serious to take the sufferer back to England - a source of great joy to the receiver and the cause of envy and admiration in his comrades. *Blighty food* was tinned food from England. A *Blighty bag*, produced in great quantities by caring ladies in England, was a cloth bag issued to the wounded at a Casualty Clearing Station for holding personal belongings once they parted company with their personal kit.

BRIGADE - Usually comprised of four battalions plus machine-guns and support units. Commanded by a Brigadier General.

BUTTE - An artificial mound on the north-east edge of Polygon Wood. Constructed originally for the musketry training of Belgian forces before 1870. The Butte was honeycombed with French and German tunnels. When taken by the Australian forces it was used as headquarters by the Australians and British. Today a memorial to the 5th Australian Division surmounts the Butte and looks out over a large British Military cemetery and a Memorial to the Missing for British and New Zealand soldiers.

CAMBRIDGE ROAD - A military name given to the road leading north from Birr Cross Roads, across the Ypres-Roulers railway where it met Railway Wood, and on to the main Ypres-Zonnebeke road between Potijze and Frezenberg.

CELTIC - A farm area and copse scattered with pill-boxes and dug-outs on the eastern slopes at the southern end of the Broodseinde Ridge.

CHATEAU WOOD - A small wood adjacent to the infamous Bellewaarde Lake, taking its name after the Château at the village of Hooge on the Menin Road and forming a part of the baronial estate.

CHINA WALL - A communication-line area made up of trenches and breastworks just east of Hell Fire Corner running south-east to the the village of Zillebeke before snaking around Halfway House and onward in an easterly direction where it fed into a military road called Oxford Street.

C.O. or **O/C** - Commanding Officer or Officer Commanding. The senior officer with responsibility for any unit. Usually a Lieutenant Colonel in a battalion or regiment.

COMMANDER-IN-CHIEF - The Commander-in-Chief was the Army's spokesman and, with his G.H.Q., the negotiator with the Secretary of State for War. The Commander-in-Chief was the only person communicating directly with the War Office. The B.E.F. was directed by the Secretary of State, but the Commander-in-Chief was always consult-ed beforehand, and always had the right of discussion and protest.

CORPS - A military formation made up from several divisions and sup-porting units with an average total strength of 40-50,000 men (see ARMY). Usually commanded by a Lieutenant General.

CYCLOPS FARM - A farm fortified by the Germans and sited east of the crest of the Broodseinde Ridge. This strongpoint would have been one of the first to fire on the advancing Australians as they crossed the ridge on 4th October 1917.

DAISY COPSE - A small wood which stood north-east of the Brood-seinde crossroads. German machine-guns positioned here were a major obstacle to the Australian advance on 4th October 1917. No trace of this wood can be found today.

D.C.M. - Distinguished Conduct Medal awarded for gallantry to non-commissioned officers and other ranks.

DEAD MANS BOTTOM - A bowl-like depression of ground immedi-ately north of Bellewaarde Lake at the village of Hooge. It was close be-hind the German front lines for two years and was an ideal location for them to muster reserves, unseen by British observers near Railway Wood.

DECLINE COPSE - Nestling alongside the bank of the old Ypres-Roulers railway line south-west of Passchendaele, this fortified copse held a commanding field of fire over the ground which the Australians had to advance in the October 1917 battles. Captain C. Jeffries V.C. 34th Batt. A.I.F. was killed by machine-gun fire from this copse in October 1917.

DEFY CROSSING - The name given to an exposed crossing where the Broodseinde-Passchendaele road met the Ypres-Roulers railway.

DIGGER - A name given to Australians and New Zealanders. Originat-ing for the Australians in the old gold-mining days at the "diggings" and for New Zealanders among the "gum-diggers". It became a title of distinc-tion in both cases. It has been said that the Australians specially claimed it for their trenching at Gallipoli, and the New Zealanders for the New Zealand Tunnelling Company operations on the Western Front. *Digger* was a common form of greeting between Australians in the Great War, as an equivalent to *Chum*. It eventually displaced *Cobber*.

DIVISION - A self-contained formation of all arms capable of independent action. A Division is an intergral unit of an Army and has in the field infantry battalions, cavalry (now tank) companies, field batteries, signallers, engineers, transport and supply services, medical and ambu-lance services. All told a Division numbered about 17,000 officers and men at the close of the war, but in 1914 the strength was nearer 20,000.

A Division is usually comprised of three brigades and commanded by a Major General.

DOCHY FARM - A large farm, north-east of Zonnebeke on the road to Langemarck. A German strongpoint captured by the 4th New Zealander Brigade on the 4th October 1917. The farm still exists today, rebuilt on its former site. It gave its name to one of the larger British military cemeteries in Belgium, sited on the other side of the road to the farm itself.

DOMINION CAMP - The heavily wooded area between Brandhoek and Poperinghe to the west of Ypres was out of range of the enemy artillery and was used by the British as an area to build camps fot the resting and recuperation of troops fresh out of the front line. Many of these camps, some hutted and some under canvas, were virtually thriving little townships with hospitals, workshops, administrative and headquarter bases, as well as areas used for sporting and other leisure activities. Some of them were quite famous due to being included on military maps. Most were serviced by the light railway systems running from Poperinghe and Ypres which were operational until just after the Second Ypres battles in 1915 when the forming of the Salient brought the German artillery into closer range. Two of the largest, mentioned in many military histories and the writings of memoirs and other such works following the war, were known as *Dirty Bucket Camp* and *Hospital Farm Camp*. *Dirty Bucket*, a literal translation of the name of an estaminet on a corner of a small crossroads north of the Poperinghe-Ypres road, was used as a name for that corner and a busy railway siding as well as the camp. *Hospital Farm Camp*, sited on another small crossroads just south-east of *Dirty Bucket Camp* also took its name from a literal translation from the French of an adjacent farm, Hôpital Ferme. The camp itself is marked on the maps of today as Hospitaalhoek (Hospital Corner). Names given to other buildings in the area testify to the "restful" nature of these camps - *Gin Palace, Cognac Cottages, Brandy House, Vermouth Villa, Booze Farm, Juice Villa. Dominion Camp* was one of the lesser known camps, and the one used by the men of the 10th Battalion A.I.F. to recuperate following the Celtic Wood raid in October 1917. It was sited south of Brandhoek on one of the railway system spurs and next to a farm given the same name. Other camps in this area give credence to its name - *Auckland, Montreal, Ottawa, Ontario, Toronto, Vancouver, Wellington etc.* The grand design and scheme of camps built up by the British around Ypres in the years 1914 to 1918 is worth a special study of its own.

D.S.O. - Distinguished Service Order. Awarded to commissioned ranks for distinguished service.

DUCKWALK TRACK - A slatted timber track laid in trenches, camps etc., and on muddy or shell-holed ground to help the movement of men, materials and transport in general. The name derives from the similarity to the sloping boards leading up to duck houses at the edge of a pond.

DUG-OUT - A protected place of shelter in the trenches, sunken roads or any other place where men could shelter from shell-fire or observation generally. Made by digging into the wall of a trench, road, slope etc. or down from the floor of the same.

FIELD AMBULANCE - A medical unit, originally comprising 241 men, of which there were three to a division. Each unit was made up of three sections, each capable of acting independently when required, comprising medical officers, stretcher-bearers, nursing orderlies, clerks, cooks etc. Each unit marched with its own brigade whose sick it was responsible for treating. A unit dealt with the evacuation of wounded from the Regimental Aid Post via the Collecting Post (usually in or near the trenches) and the Advanced Dressing Station back to the Main Dressing Station, run by another of the Ambulances. From here Divisional treatment ceased and the wounded were transferred to the Motor Ambulance Convey, administered by Corps, and carried back to the Casualty Clearing Station, whence by ambulance train, they went to base hospitals and, from there, by hospital ship to the U.K. The third unit of the Divisional Field Ambulances usually ran a Walking Wounded Collecting Station in the neighbourhood of the Main or Advanced Dressing Station.

FIELD GUN - A mobile gun or cannon used on the battlefield for low-trajectory, high velocity fire.

FIELD MARSHAL - Highest ranking officer in the British Army, equivalent to a naval Admiral of the Fleet

FLINTE FARM - A fortified farm and copse garrisoned by German infantry just north-east of Celtic on the eastern slopes of the Broodseinde Ridge. Traces of pill-box remains can still be seen in the small copse today and the small water channel used by the Germans as a water supply now serves to irrigate the nearby field and to slake the thirst of cattle.

G.H.Q. - General Headquarters, from where the war was conducted, housed the Commander-in-Chief and his staff. During the Great War it was set-up in Montreuil on March 31st 1916 when the original headquarter town of St. Omer was felt no longer suitable. General Headquarters was the link between the Army and the British Government as well as between the Army and the Allied Armies. It decided the strategy of the war. It arranged the supply of all the needs of the Army from tanks to cigarettes, managed a transport system to meet this supply as well as for the movement of men. It was responsible for building roads, railways and harbour facilities, it ran canal and sea services, forestry and agricultural services, repair shops, laundries, and managed medical services, vetinary services, laboratories etc., and was also responsible for religious and educational facilities. General Headquarters was never intended to be a great military camp. It never exceeded 5,000, including troops who were needed as guards and who were drawn from the Artists Rifles, then from the Honourable Artillery Company, the Newfoundland Regiment and finally the Guernsey Regiment.

GLENCORSE WOOD - A small wood just south-west of Polygon Wood and north of the Menin Road. The Royal Scots named it after their depôt in Glencorse barracks. Filled with small forts and pill-boxes it saw heavy fighting in 1917 being reached by the 18th Division on the 31st July and captured by the 1st Australian Division on 20th September.

GRENADE - A hand-thrown bomb.

GUNNER - A member of a gun team. R.F.A., R.H.A., R.G.A.

HALFWAY HOUSE - A ruined farm with spacious cellars used as a headquarters by various units. Sited south of Hell Fire Corner and close to Zillebeke in the China Wall area it was also used by ration and carrier parties. Still in the same position today, the reconstructed farm was built over its original cellars.

HAMBURG - A fortified farm close to that of Beecham on the rise to the Tyne Cot Defence line. Easily identifiable today as, when standing at the gates of Tyne Cot with the cemetery to the back, it stands approximately 400 metres half-right on the ground opposite.

HELL FIRE CORNER - An exposed crossing at the point where the old Ypres-Roulers railway crossed the Menin Road just east of the town of Ypres at the crossroads with the Zillebeke-Potijze road. On a board a yard long was painted in white letters on black "To Hell Fire Corner". In 1915 Canadian troops placed this board at the Menin Gate in Ypres and it stayed there until the end of the war. The name became official and started to appear on military maps. Until July 1917 this board marked the limit for all transport at night. German artillery always had Hell Fire Corner accurately targeted and were able to maintain constant observation from the high ground they held on the Hooge Ridge. For this reason long "walls" of hessian strip were constructed to mask observation from enemy gunners. Hell Fire Corner was the place most soldiers never wanted to visit, whereas today it is the place that most battlefield visitors want to visit. It is a busy spot today but well worth taking the time to stop and reflect upon all that happened on and around this most famous of corners.

HELLES RIDGE - High ground north of Polygon Wood. A main Australian supply route to the Broodseinde Ridge in September and October 1917. A name with sacred memories of the Australian and British experiences at Gallipoli.

HILLSIDE FARM - As its name implies, a fortified farm on the hillside just north of Tyne Cot, close to Defy Crossing and Decline Copse and in sight of Passchendaele village itself. Several large pill-boxes dominated this position and it was while attacking this defence line that Captain Clarence Jeffries of the 34th Battalion A.I.F. won his Victoria Cross. A large portion of a wall of one of the bigger pill-boxes lies on its side in the garden of a small house sited on the old farm house and a water pump close to it identifies the position of the garrison water source that once was inside the structure.

HOOGE CRATER - A large British mine crater blown in July 1915 at Hooge Château in the village of Hooge on the Menin Road. Now an ornamental pond in the old Château grounds, the crater, with pill-boxes still mounting its edge, faces a military cemetery carrying the same name on the opposite side of the road.

THE HUTS - A hutted camp near the village of Dickebusch in an area sited with many battery positions. Now the site of a British Military Cemetery of the same name in a secondary country road about half-a-mile north-west of Dickebusch and four miles south-west of Ypres. The Ypres-Dickebusch road carried a constant stream of artillery traffic and about two-thirds of those buried at The Huts Military cemetery are gunners, underlying the importance of this district to the artillery during the war.

KEIBURG SPUR - A major German defence position east of the Broodseinde Ridge. It was only ever attacked during the final allied offensive in 1918. Some skirmishes took place here in 1914 when the 2nd Division tried to stem the German move on Ypres. Prince Maurice of Battenberg, Kings Royal Rifle Corps, was mortally wounded at the Keiburg Spur in October 1914. He lies in the Ypres Town British cemetery.

LAST POST - Originally part of Tattoo, the name for the party sent round a military garrison beating drums to notify troops that all must return to quarters for the night. The drum-beat as the party fell-in to start Tattoo was called *First Post* and the final drum-beat when they returned to the starting point was called *Last Post*. Now a bugle-call that orders men to retire to sleep or, more emotively, a bugle-call sounded at military funerals or ceremonies in respect of the fallen.

MENIN GATE - The exit through the Ypres ramparts leading directly onto the road to the German occupied town of Menin - the Menin Road.

This exit from the town of Ypres was that most exposed to German observation points. Constantly under shellfire this "gate", marked by a statue of a lion on either side of the road as it passed through the famous Vauban Ramparts, was known by every serving soldier as a place of menace and danger to be avoided at all costs and, as war would have it, almost unavoidable to those who served in the Salient. A memorial to the British dead of 1914-1918 who have no known graves was erected during the twenties and officially inaugurated the 24th July 1927. From that date, except for the period of the second world war, traffic has been stopped on the road through this now impressive "gate" or arch for the sounding of the Last Post, played on silver bugles by members of the Ypres fire-brigade. Originally designed to carry 60,000 names, it was not large enough to record all the missing. To complete the toll the screened walls of Tyne Cot Military Cemetery were so designed to carry the remainder. The original statues of the lions that once straddled this ominous exit to the battlefields of the Ypres Salient now reside in the Canberra War Museum in Australia.

MENIN ROAD - The road linking the town of Ypres with that of Menin to the east. This road is often referred to as the *Voie Sacré* of the British Army.

MENTIONED IN DESPATCHES - A recognition of an act of bravery, but not an official award. Lieutenant Scott, 10th Batallion A.I.F. who led the raid on Celtic Wood, together with several of his men, were Mentioned in Despatches following the operation.

MILITARY CROSS (M.C.) - British Military medal for gallantry - awarded to commissioned ranks. As an award, it ranks below the D.S.O.

MILITARY MEDAL (M.M.) - British Military medal for gallantry - awarded to non-commissioned officers and other ranks.

MOLENAARELSTHOEK - A small hamlet on the western slope near the crest of the Broodseinde ridge which was fiercely defended by the Germans and described at the time as " full of pill-boxes and small forts". Celtic Wood lay approximately four hundred metres away, over the ridge on the eastern slope.

N.C.O. - Non-commissioned officer.

NO-MANS LAND - The dividing strip of land between the allied and enemy front line positions. Constantly patrolled, fought for and raided over by both sides. Although recorded in use as early as AD 1320, and as "recently" as 1881 and 1890, it was coined when the Great War became one of entrenchment, and first appeared in print in an *Eyewitness* narrative on 15th September 1915. *Eyewitness* was an unofficial name given to the official correspondent with the British Expeditionary Force in France who supplied the British public with what information the authorities thought fit to allow them.

OTHER RANKS - The usual official designation for non-commissioned officers and private soldiers.

PILL-BOX - The name from the shape, often circular in plan, of the German ferro-concrete, small battlefield redoubts or forts employed from the Autumn of 1917 in Flanders to defend sections of the line. Some of the larger were quadrangular in shape. They were garrisoned by small detatchments of infantry with machine-guns and were proof against anything except a direct hit by a shell from a big gun. The German term for these structures was MEBU, the abbreviation of *Maschinengewehr-Eisenbeton-Unterstand* - Machine-Gun-Iron-Concrete-Emplacement.

POLYGON WOOD - A cluster of woods incorporated into the German line between Zonnebeke and Hooge were named *Nonne Boschen, Glencorse* and *Polygon*. The latter, and largest taking its name from a translation of the Flemish *Polygonveld* and the French *Polygone de Zonnebeke*. All lay to the north of of the Menin Road with the leafy mass of *Polygon Wood* easily seen on the high ground north of the village of Gheluvelt. The wood contained many rides and fire "alleys" which disected it rather like a grid system. In the middle of the wood was a trotting course and at the north-eastern end was incorporated an artificial mound, the Butte, used for pre-war musketry practice by the Belgian infantry. The many rides were used as a training area for the Belgian Cavalry (see BUTTE). In September 1917 *Polygon Wood* was a major obstacle and a tough nut to crack for the British attackers. It lay in the path of II Anzac Corps and the British 3rd Division on their left during the the succesful attack in taking Zonnebeke and the ground in front of the Broodseinde Ridge.

RAILWAY WOOD - A small wood on the *Cambridge Road* north of Birr Cross Roads. Named in April 1915 after its proximity to the Ypres-Roulers railway, the British front line ran through it for over two years. For many of the post war years the memorial to the 14th Light Division, who held the line here in 1915 through the infamous "liquid fire" attacks, stood in the wood. It was removed to its present site at Hill 60 in 1978 by members of the Rifle Brigade depôt at Winchester. This move was necessitated by the ground below the memorial breaking up due the existence of the old British tunnels and mining systems workings dug beneath it.

REMI SIDINGS - A railway siding complex near the village of Lijssenthoek just south of Poperinghe used for the evacuation of the wounded from local hospitals to the coast. Named after the farm standing aside the railway, Remi Sidings is the name generally used for Lijssenthoek British Military Cemetery which is sited on the other side of the farm to what was once the railway. The farm is still there and still carries the Flemish name *Remi Hoeve*, but a two-lane road has replaced the old railway and has been built atop the original embankment. Lijssenthoek (Remi Sidings) British Military Cemetery is second only to Tyne Cot in size and number of graves.

REMUS WOOD - A ruined wood just west of the Broodseinde ridge crest. Well fortified by the Germans and an important sector of their defence lines.

RETALIATION FARM - A fortified farm in the valley west of the Broodseinde ridge and just south of Zonnebeke lake. This farm and its surrounding area saw much of the close combat fighting between Australians and Germans at dawn on the 4th October 1917. The name *Retaliation* however was originated before the October battles and appears on battle maps of the 1914-15 period.

R.F.A. - Royal Field Artillery.

R.G.A. - Royal Garrison Artillery.

R.H.A. - Royal Horse Artillery.

ROMULUS WOOD - A twin of Remus Wood and sited very close by.

S.A.A. - Small-Arms Ammunition. Ammunition for rifles, machine-guns and revolvers.

SALIENT - A curve in the line of battle, projecting toward or into the enemy's line.

SANCTUARY WOOD - A large woodland lying just south of the Menin Road at Hooge. *Sanctuary* was the name given to it when cavalry and other units before the First Battle of Ypres in 1914 used its confines as a place of shelter. It was first shelled in November of 1914, was the scene of heavy fighting in 1915 and was the centre of the Battle of Mount Sorrel in the first two weeks of June 1916

SPOILBANK - This was an area of heaped spoil excavated during the construction of the Ypres-Comines canal and given the name by army cartographers as an easily identifiable position south of Ypres. It was in British hands for the whole period of the war and used as a haven of shelter, safe from shelling. It housed headquarters of various units operating in the area, aid stations, sleeping quarters etc. Later in the war it was reported that an excellent and highly efficient underground electric lighting system was installed and a well equipped hospital built within its depths. In 1940 it sprang into brief prominence again when a British force, under the soon to become Field Marshal Montgomery, brilliantly defended this area against overwhelming German forces to help keep open for many critical hours one of the main B.E.F. escape routes to Dunkirk. Many casualties from 1940 now lie peacefully amongst their compatriots from an earlier war.

SUPPORTS - Troops maintained immediately behind the firing-line for the purpose of re-inforcement in attack or defence.

SUPPORT TRENCH - A trench immediately behind the front fire-trench.

TAPES - The tapes laid down to give alignment or direction to troops moving to, or forming, an attack.

TOKIO SPUR - Named after the German pill-box sited on this small ridge immediately south of Zonnebeke village. TOKIO Spur was one of the objectives of the abortive German counter-attack at dawn on 4th October 1917.

TOWER HAMLETS - An imposing escarpment of high ground just south of the Menin Road, also known as the Gheluvelt Plateau after the name of the tactically important village of Gheluvelt sited there. Its height, which gave the occupiers such comprehensive observation, together with an imposing row of pill-boxes, enabled the German defences in this area to withstand all British efforts to take it during the Passchendaele battles. It only ever fell into British hands during the German retreat in 1918. The name *Tower Hamlets* was accorded to this part of the Salient from the earliest period of the fighting around Ypres during 1914-15 and was probably designated as such by troops from London who identified it with that area of East London with the same name. Army map makers did the rest and the name became the official designation for this part of the Salient throughout the war.

TRENCH - A defensive work dug into the ground by troops working from the surface.

TRENCH MORTAR - A light form of short range artillery, firing a light, medium or heavy thin-walled bomb which contains explosive in high proportion to its weight.

TYNE COT - Popularly thought to have been named by Northumbrian Fusiliers troops during the Second Battle of Ypres in April 1915. Story has it that his part of the Passchendaele Ridge with its vast number of squat pill-boxes, situated near a level crossing on the Passchendaele-Broodseinde road, reminded them of of Tyne Cottages in England and the Army map service staff officialised the name. This is hardly likely as pill-boxes in vast numbers in this area came as quite a suprise to the the British Army during Third Ypres in 1917. It is more likely, according to the locals, that Tyne Cot is the British soldiers' spelling and pronunciation of the local Flemish spoken dialect for *het hennekot* (hen or chicken house) which, with the common usage of *het* as *'t* and the use of a silent *h*, is pronounced *'t hennekot*. Tyne Cot is the largest British military cemetery in the world and its Memorial to the Missing records the names of 34,957 men with no known graves.

V.C. (The Victoria Cross) - The British Empire's highest award for gallantry and valour in battle. The award is only given for an officially witnessed act of gallantry. The crosses are made from the bronze of Russian guns captured at Sevastopol in the Crimean War. Records bulge with instances where it was thought a particular act deserved the award, but when an officer of sufficient rank was not present to bear witness. A noteworthy case was that of Robert Graves (writer and poet) who made it quite clear that he felt his son, a Major fighting in Burma in 1944, deserved the award. He never forgave the military authorities for failing to agree with him. Major Graves was killed in action fighting the Japanese.

YPRES SALIENT - The British defence line formed around the Belgian town of Ypres after the 1915 battles. Constantly under attack, and defended at enormous cost in men and materials, the *Immortal Salient* was never pierced by the German Armies.

FIRST BATTLE OF YPRES (First Ypres) - **Oct. to Nov. 1914.**
Following the British retreat from Mons and the later offensive battles moving them northwards in what was sometimes referred to as "the race to the sea" the British Expeditionary Force fought the Germans to the north, east and south of Ypres, defending and holding this strategically important town to save the channel ports. This battle line was the forerunner to the Ypres Salient which was formulated in 1915.

The First Ypres battle major actions were :
a) Langemarck, 21st - 24th October.
b) Gheluvelt, 29th -31st October.
c) Nonne Bosschen, 11th November.

SECOND BATTLE OF YPRES (Second Ypres) - **April to May 1915.**
Ypres was defended and held again, and the Ypres Salient was formed. The German army's use of their new forms of 'ammunition', gas and liquid fire, notorised this period.

The Second Ypres battle major actions were :
a) Battle of Gravenstafel, 22nd - 23rd April.
b) Battle of St. Julien, 24th April - 4th May.
c) Battle of Frezenberg, 8th - 13th May.
d) Battle of Bellewaarde, 24th - 25th May.

THIRD BATTLE OF YPRES (Third Ypres) - July to Nov. 1917.
The British attempt to break out of the Salient and establish a sound winter line. Battlefield conditions were abyssmal but Passchendaele fell to the Canadian Corps in November and, with the capture of the ridge, the battle closed down for the winter.

The Third Ypres battle major actions were :

a) Battle of Pilckem, 31st July - 2nd August.

b) Battle of Langemarck, 16th - 18th August.

c) Battle of the Menin Road, 20th - 25th September

d) Battle of Polygon Wood, 26th September - 3rd October.

e) Battle of Broodseinde, 4th October.

f) Battle of Poelcappelle, 9th October.

g) First Passchendaele, 12th October.

h) Second Passchendaele, 26th October - 10th November.

ZOUAVE WOOD - A small copse linked to Sanctuary Wood just south of the village of Hooge on the Menin Road. Named in 1914 when a battalion of French Colonial troops, Zouaves, used it as a bivouac area. The British front line ran through here from 1915 until the spring of 1918 and it was near this wood that the Germans introduced "liquid fire". It was following this "liquid fire" attack that the Rifle Brigade mounted the abortive counter-attack attempting to recapture the village of Hooge in July of 1915.

BIBLIOGRAPHY

Military Operations, France & Belgium Vol. II. 1917. Brigadier General Sir James Edmonds. (HMSO 1948).

The Story of Anzac. Volume I. C. E. W. Bean. (Angus & Robertson, Sydney 1921).

Australia in the Great War. France Volume IV. 1917. C. E. W. Bean. (Angus & Robertson, Sydney 1943).

Sir Douglas Haig's Despatches. (J. H. Boraston 1919)

The 10th A.I.F. 1914-18. (Cassell & Co. Ltd.1919).

War Diary 1st Australian Division. (W/O 95/3159).

War Diary 3rd Australian Division. (W/O 95/3243).

War Diary 10th Australian Battalion. (W/O 95/3248).

Randwick to Hargicourt. The History of the 3rd Battalion A.I.F. Eric Wren. (Ronald McDonald, Sydney, Australia 1935).

War letters from General Monash. (Angus & Robertson Ltd. 1934).

Der Weltrieg 1914-1918. General Von Kuhl. (Weller, Berlin 1920).

1914-1918. General E. Ludendorff. (Hutchison 1919).

Flanderen, 1917. W. Beumelberg. (Oldenburg : Stalling 1928).

Author's papers. Colonel Rory Macleod. D.S.O., M.C. (1978).

Author's papers. John Laffin. (1989).

Road to Passchendaele. John Terraine. (Leo Cooper 1977).

Haig Diaries. John Terraine papers.

At G.H.Q.1914-1918. Brigadier General John Charteris. C.M.G., D.S.O. (Cassel & Co. Ltd. 1931).

G.H.Q. (Montreuil-sur-mer). "G.S.O." (Philip Allan & Co. 1920).

The V.C. and D.S.O. Volume I. Sir O'Moore Creagh, V.C., G.C.B., G.C.S.I. and E. M. Humphris. (The Standard Art Book Co. Ltd. 1924)

The Great War - Volume III. The Right Honourable Winston S. Churchill. (George Newnes Ltd.).

In Flanders Fields. Leon Wolfe. (Longman & Green, London 1958).

Passchendaele and the Somme. Hugh Quigley. (Methuen & Co. Ltd. 1928).

Warrior. Lieutenant Colonel Graham Seton Hutchison. D.S.O., M.M. (Hutchison & Co. Ltd. 1932).

A Fatalist at War. Rudolf Binding. (George Allen & Unwin 1929).

The Immortal Heritage. Fabian Ware. Edmund Blunden. (Cambridge University Press 1937).

Ypres, Then and Now. John Giles. (Leo Cooper 1975).

The Immortal Salient. Lieutenant General Sir William Pulteney and Beatrix Price. Sir Philip Gibbs. K.B.E. (John Murray 1925).

A Medico's Luck in the Great War . Colonel David Rorie. D.S.O., T.D., M.D., D.P.H. (Milne & Hutchison. Aberdeen 1929).

The Silent Cities. Sidney C. Hurst. P.A.S.I. (Methuen & Co. Ltd. 1929).

Soldier and Sailor Words and Phrases. Edward Fraser and John Gibbons. (George Routledge and Sons Ltd. 1926).

Songs and Slang of the British Soldier 1914-1918. J. Brophey and E. Patridge. (Eric Partridge Ltd. 1930).

Canadian Expeditionary Force 1914-1919. Official History of the Canadian Army in the First World War. Colonel G. W. L. Nicholson (Queens Printer, Ottawa, 1962).

The Empire at War vol. II. Prof. F. H. Underhill, edited by Sir Charles Lucas. (Oxford University Press 1921).